Beth has written this transformative book in a way that you feel her closely alongside you, guiding you with care, humour and deep insight through the WorkJoy Toolkit. This is a pragmatic, perspective shifting read that invites reflection and offers highly effective exercises along the way. I really appreciated the relational lens through which Beth views our wellbeing at work, and the empowerment she encourages through empathy and accountability. Here is an enlightening and inspirational guide that is sure to ignite joy and unleash potential.

Ruth Coates, psychotherapist and therapeutic writing guide

This book is essential reading for the modern workplace – leaders and staff alike. It cuts right to the heart of what is affecting people in careers around the world and how a 'job' is just one part of bringing balance and happiness to work. Pick this up, take control of your choices, and see the difference you can make. There is not a perfect career or a linear path to get one, but this book will help you or your team navigate it.

Matt Jowett, Head of Transformation Delivery and Comms – Foreign Commonwealth and Development Office

Having worked with Beth for many years, I've always marvelled at her ability to bring both pragmatism and positivity to any situation, however complex. The genius of WorkJoy is understanding that with practice and by being more purposeful in our pursuit of fulfilment at work we can all learn to be more like Beth. For me, WorkJoy has made a huge difference to the way I approach work and it's something I'm grateful for on a daily basis.

Jo Smallwood, Head of Learning and Development – Soldo

In this book, Beth has taken a complex and elusive topic, the pursuit of a better, joyful working life, and has written a powerful guide to making this happen in your own life. Beth's way of thinking and writing is incredibly engaging – from the sharply defined concepts to the practical solutions. From the questions for reflection to my favourite parts of the book, the mental models and the visual depictions that light up my brain. It's shifted the way I work. The way I lead. And even the way I think. This is more than a toolkit for a better working life. It's a full yet fun-filled manual for creating a better LIFE.

Chet Morjaria, business and communications coach, co-founder of Impact Accelerator, and author of *Work Worth Doing*

This book is truly joyous and uplifting! It's full of practical tips to help us take a proactive approach to creating a more fulfilling life at work and beyond. There is something for every reader whatever your chosen profession and whatever stage of career you're at, and a useful reminder that whilst we can't always control outcomes, we can choose to make the journey and experience of our working lives more joyful.

Dr Cath Bishop, Olympian, former diplomat, leadership and culture coach and consultant, author of *The Long Win*

Sometimes a book comes along which is one of those that you will continue to pick up and dive into long after the first read. Beth has brilliantly brought together both the art and science of making work better each day in a way that is both instantly relatable and readily transferable.

Kate Goodger, PhD C. Psychol, Group Head of Human Innovation and Performance – Laing O'Rourke

A toolkit for a better working life

Beth Stallwood

Want to bulk-buy copies of this book for your team and colleagues? We can introduce case studies, customize the content and co-brand *WorkJoy* to suit your business's needs.

Please email info@practicalinspiration.com for more details.

To my parents, who always encouraged me to 'do what you love'.

TABLE OF CONTENTS

INTRODUCTION

As you'll see a bit later, stories are an essential part of being human. I'd like to open this toolkit by telling you mine…

My WorkJoy story

I sat in the living room, staring out of the window. I'd been up since the early hours of the morning, too excited to sleep. Then there it was, a white Mercedes pulling into the driveway. It was 1990 and this was a very fancy car, with a driver, coming to take me to my first ever paid job (at the tender age of 8). I'd been given special permission to be off school and I was ready to burst. My Mum and I jumped in, and we headed off to Pinewood Studios.

I toured the sound stages and water tanks where some of the greatest movies had been shot. Then I was ushered to my dressing room where the new outfit that the costume designer and I had chosen a few weeks before was awaiting me (it included a pair of red converse high tops – the height of fashion!). I got changed and they did my hair and make-up. Then I headed to our set and spent two days filming with three grown-up actors. After which, my first ever paid gig was complete and I headed home, back to school and back to normal life.

Up at the crack of dawn one Saturday morning months later, I wandered downstairs and turned on the TV. Hearing a very loud scream, my parents ran downstairs to find out what was wrong. It was all over, 30 seconds gone. I had just watched myself on TV for the first time. Multiple auditions, rehearsals, and two days of filming condensed into one very short commercial for Heinz Tomato Ketchup.[1] Luckily my parents didn't have to wait long as it was on a lot in the first few years of the 1990s. I later discovered that this is not the standard introduction to work that most people experience. Chauffeur-driven cars, being given a year's supply of red sauce, and being allowed to keep the outfit are not the norm. Yet it sparked in me a real love for working that hasn't stopped – even with the very much less glamorous work I've done since!

When I was in my teens, I envisaged my career on the West End stage, being a fighter pilot in the RAF (influenced heavily by Top Gun!) or being the conductor at the Last Night of the Proms. I dreamt big and was supported by parents who told me I could do anything I set my mind to. I always had one thing at the core of what I wanted to do, and I remember an event that nailed this down. I was about 15 and rehearsing for a play with my amateur dramatics group. The director, whom I'd known forever, asked me this question: 'What Do You Want to Be When You Grow Up?'

It's a question every young person has been asked at some point in their life. I thought for a moment, and I responded with one word: **Happy**. He was taken aback. He was expecting me to announce my career intent. He smiled and said, 'good choice'. We sadly lost him to Covid, but he will live in my memory as one of the first people to help me define what was to come twenty-something years later. I didn't know it at the time, but I had stated my intent to focus on **joy**.

---

[1] *Heinz Tomato Ketchup advert.* YouTube (Piker Ads channel) (uploaded 26 November 2007). Available from: www.youtube.com/watch?v=OLk9LpFoJIM [accessed 25 August 2022].

From being a barmaid, to fitting kids' shoes, my early career is not so different from many others. I enjoyed having purpose beyond going to lectures, reading, rehearsing, and writing essays when I was studying. Once I'd graduated and realized that a degree in music wasn't the most career-forming option, I decided to get a temp job until I had worked out what to do. From that, an unexpected career formed. I found myself training, coaching, and leading teams in financial services. I then moved to the public sector for a couple of years and my last employed job was as a head of talent and development in the world of sport. The theme of my work has always been people and enabling them to perform at their best.

Since 2017, I've worked independently as a consultant, speaker, coach, and facilitator across a range of industries and organizations, from small start-ups to tech scale-ups, sports, universities, and corporates. Through every role, every step-up, and every organization I've worked with, I've been able to create and cultivate joy. Even when times have been tough, when hurdles were in the way, and when I couldn't quite see the light at the end of the tunnel, I found the route through. I can honestly say I have loved every single job I have ever done. None of them have been perfect. They have all been wonderful in their own way.

Working with such a diverse range of organizations and thousands of people has given me deep insight into what brings people joy at work, and the things that have the opposite effect. I've worked with organizations to create working environments that encourage a better working life. I've coached leaders to enable them to engage and support their people in a positive way. I've supported individuals to take control of their working life, crafting careers that give them what they want and need.

There is no single route to a more joyful working life. There are many options, choices, and challenges along the way. I have distilled my two decades of experience into a toolkit that will enable you to chart your own course for more joy.

About this toolkit

You may have picked up this book as you wandered around the book shop, and you liked the cover? Perhaps it was recommended to you by a colleague or friend? Maybe it popped up online and the title intrigued you, so you downloaded the e-book? Whichever way this toolkit came to you, let me share more about who it's for and how to utilize it for maximum impact. This isn't a theoretical or academic study (if that's your bag, this might not be right for you). It's a collection of tried and tested practical tools gathered from years of working with people like you. It's designed to take you on an expedition to find and maintain more joy in your working life.

Who is this book for?

This book is for you if you're ready to take personal responsibility for increasing your levels of joy at work.

- Perhaps you're feeling a bit stuck and looking for ways to move beyond the stickiness?
- Maybe you're at a career crossroads and seeking inspiration on what's next?
- Or have you fallen out of love with a job you once adored and want to rekindle that spark?
- Are you already feeling some joy and want to supercharge it, getting more of it, more often?

Whatever your starting point, whether it's a massive change or a little nudge you need, this book can help. By engaging with the process, investing some energy, and being ready to experiment, you'll make the most of this toolkit.

What is covered in this book?

Part 1: About WorkJoy and WorkGloom

- This section (chapter 1) provides the foundation for understanding the concept of WorkJoy through **WorkJoy definitions**, the **WorkJoy formulae**, and the **WorkJoy mindset**.

Part 2: The inner WorkJoy factors

- This section dives into your mindset about WorkJoy and WorkGloom and encourages you to consider these from different viewpoints. These inner factors are mainly within your control, they're the things you can do for yourself.
- From how work fits into your **Life** (chapter 2), to understanding the **Values** you hold deeply (chapter 3). Then working out the **Boundaries** that are important to you (chapter 4) and exploring the **Stories** you tell yourself and others (chapter 5). You'll end this section discovering what your approach to **Learning** is (chapter 6).

Part 3: The outer WorkJoy factors

- This section explores different sources of WorkJoy and WorkGloom and provides tools for how to navigate them. Some of these factors are outside of your control, yet most are influenceable when you take personal responsibility.
- From the people who help you in your **Squads** (chapter 7), to the shape of your **Careers** (chapter 8). To

considering the relationship with the **Organizations** you work with (chapter 9) and the **Bosses** that lead you (chapter 10).

Part 4: Making it happen

- This section is focused on action, crafting goals, building helpful habits, and overcoming hurdles. It's where you'll turn thinking into action.
- From setting **Goals** to set you on a path to progress (chapter 11) to making **Choices** (the conclusion).

How does this toolkit work?

This toolkit can be used in two ways:

- You can read it from beginning to end, starting with the foundations (WorkJoy and WorkGloom), and working through the practical advice step-by-step – the full immersion experience!
- You could also choose to focus on the sections that appeal to your needs right now – the 'pick and mix' experience! I'd suggest that you read **Part 1: About WorkJoy and WorkGloom** first. This will make sure you have a good grounding in the WorkJoy concepts, mindset, and formulae before you head off on your self-led expedition.

Throughout the toolkit, you'll see three features pop up regularly:

 Reflection questions: At these moments, I'd encourage you to pause, consider, and reflect on the questions. They are designed to help you personalize the content to your unique experience, situation, and style. For some, the answers may quickly come to mind. For others of you, it may require some deeper thought, perhaps with a pen and paper (or digital alternative) to make some notes for yourself.

 WorkJoy WorkBook: To support this toolkit, I have created a downloadable PDF which will help you work through exercises and experiments suggested. It has step-by-step instructions and templates. You can download this for *free* at https://createworkjoy.com/workbook.

 WorkJoy stories: Throughout the toolkit you'll read stories from people just like you who have invested in this approach and have reaped the benefits of cultivating more WorkJoy.

Getting started

In whichever way you choose to use this toolkit, I hope it helps you to create and cultivate more joy in your working life. Let's begin by exploring more about what WorkJoy means.

PART 1

ABOUT WORKJOY
AND WORKGLOOM

CHAPTER 1

THE FOUNDATIONS

Introduction

You bought this book (thanks!), so I already know you want more WorkJoy. But what is WorkJoy really? What is it not? And – just as important – what's left behind when WorkJoy has well and truly vacated the premises? In this chapter, you'll cover the basics, including how to spot WorkJoy (it can hide in plain sight), how to visualize it and make it your everyday mindset. I'll also introduce you to my tried and tested WorkJoy formulae. Let's get going and start with what WorkJoy is.

Defining WorkJoy

Work and Joy. These two words are rarely seen or spoken about in the same sentence, so let's start with the definitions:

> **WorkJoy (noun):** *the positive, warm, or happy feeling you get about your work, when working or at your workplace*

A noun is a little too passive. WorkJoy needs to be active and, therefore, it must be a verb!

> **WorkJoy (verb):** *to develop the mindset and take action in pursuit of a better working life*

WorkJoy is something you feel on the inside that shows on the outside too. That warm feeling translates to a real smile, a positive tone in your voice and a little skip in your step. It stems from a hopeful place where you feel positive and energized. It builds your courage and makes you feel able to take on work-related challenges.

Sources of WorkJoy?

The sources of WorkJoy are varied and depend on individual preferences, ranging from micro to massive and from minor to major in terms of their impact. It might be helpful to consider them in three buckets:

Micro-moments	These are the little moments that really add up. Ticking off an item on a to-do list, a colleague saying hello, or starting a fresh notepad. These fleeting moments of joy are just as important as the big things. They are also a great place to start when building your approach; they are easy to introduce and build great momentum.
Personal preferences	These are dependent on your style in any situation. You might feel joy from presenting to your team, or that might fill you with utter dread. Perhaps you attend some meetings that are inspiring, yet others leave you wanting to sit in a darkened room. There are likely some people at work that light you up and others that suck the positivity out of you (you'll look at this more in chapter 7 – **Squads**). It is not the situation but the combination of factors that define whether it's a joyful experience for you.

Fundamental factors	These are the unwieldy things like purpose, leadership, and organizational culture. These factors are more complex, yet, when boiled down to their component parts, they are simply the accumulation of small actions and behaviours. Things that happen regularly, and are adopted by the majority, becoming part of how things are spoken about and the 'way things are done around here'. If, for example, there is a mismatch between your organization's culture and your preferences (see chapter 9 – **Organizations**), you may be facing an uphill battle to find joy.

Luckily, sources of WorkJoy are plentiful and they have the habit of multiplying. The combination of factors, sources, and actions that bring you WorkJoy on a consistent basis will be unique to you. Copying someone else's approach may give you inspiration, yet not quite hit the mark for your circumstances, style, and approach. The things that bring you WorkJoy may also change over time. Different roles bring different opportunities, changing life stages may require you to re-prioritize, and organizations will present you with a variety of challenges. Being prepared to flex and adapt is how you build a sustainable approach.

Defining WorkGloom

The opposite of WorkJoy is WorkGloom, which can be defined as:

WorkGloom (noun): *the negative, sad, or frustrated feeling you get about your work, when working or at your workplace*

You experience the gloominess often (not always) because you're not taking the appropriate actions to change the situation, or your habits have led you down a gloomy path. WorkGloom isn't something you can simply pass off as something someone else or an organization has created for you. Apportioning blame without taking personal responsibility is a passive way of dealing with the gloom. Let's action this up instead and create a verb definition!

> **WorkGloom (verb):** *to adopt and embed the unhelpful habits that lead you into a downward spiral of work-based negativity that spills over into your life beyond work*

WorkGloom is a place of passiveness and/or negativity, that makes you feel bad on the inside. It stifles your energy and passion for work. In its mild version it could be described as feeling a bit 'meh' and in its chronic version as crushing. It shows on the outside too, translating to a resting gloom face, a moany tone in your voice, and perhaps a physical change in your posture.

Sources of WorkGloom?

Sources of WorkGloom range from seemingly trivial (yet horribly impactful) things like 'someone didn't smile at me today', to bigger things like leadership and communication. Unfortunately, sources of WorkGloom are also plentiful (the harsh truth!). What gets you riled-up will be unique to you, although there are many recurring themes. Some sources of WorkGloom are the things that happen to you, and some you may create for yourself. Your quest with WorkGloom is to learn strategies, techniques, and habits that tame and manage it.

What WorkJoy isn't about

You're not in control of 100% of the things that happen in your life, so your goal is not to rid yourself of gloom entirely.

That's a fool's errand and anyone who's seen *Inside Out* by Disney's Pixar will understand the trouble it causes! There are always going to be things that you don't enjoy at work. From annoying policies to frustrating people and technology trying your patience, you can't fix everything. You will, over time, be able to notice these irritants and reduce their impact.

WorkJoy isn't about being happy all the time, plastering a fake smile on your face or never feeling frustrated. That's called toxic positivity[2] and it's worse than WorkGloom. There will be times when you feel rubbish. Part of creating a better working life for yourself is accepting that fact and working through the emotion – not trying to circumnavigate it. Gloom often comes over you when something has got you down, when there's not been enough counterbalancing joy, or even when your attempts to change have not gone to plan. Allowing yourself a bad day (or two) to feel all the emotions is important. A short wallow is allowed. The bad days are useful insights to help you understand where the edges of your WorkGloom are and can spur you on to put helpful habits in place.

Beyond WorkGloom

WorkJoy isn't about passively accepting a toxic work environment, believing that everything that isn't right is somehow your fault, or continuing to be treated poorly in your workplace. If you're ever feeling bullied, harassed, or unsafe, if you're experiencing discrimination, or if there are unchallenged inappropriate behaviours happening in your organization, that's not okay and it will not be fixed by embarking on a WorkJoy quest.

---

[2] S. Quintero and J. Long, *Toxic positivity: The dark side of positive vibes*. The Psychology Group Fort Lauderdale. Available from: https://thepsychologygroup.com/toxic-positivity/ [accessed 25 July 2022].

These factors go beyond the usual annoyances and frustrations that work brings. They describe an unhealthy workplace culture. If you're stuck in a situation, please talk to someone you trust about these issues. Your initial efforts may be best spent addressing these issues or finding somewhere different to work where you and your individual brilliance are valued.

A note on mental health

Mental health is at the heart of being able to embark on, and benefit from, your personal WorkJoy journey. If you are reading this and are experiencing any mental health issues or feel that your levels of gloom have moved beyond the standard challenges that we all experience from time to time, please do consult a mental health professional. This book is not intended as a solution or treatment to mental health issues or mental illness.

Understanding WorkJoy over time

It can help to visualize what WorkJoy might look like in the real world over a period. This diagram shows an example of an average working week plotted with WorkJoy and WorkGloom moments. You'll also see there's a central area entitled the **neutral zone**. Not everything that happens in a day will fit at the elation or misery end of the spectrum. For much of the time, you're likely to be betwixt the two!

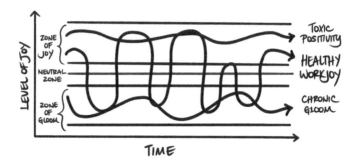

Healthy WorkJoy

Here you can see the ebb and flow of joy and gloom, moving through the neutral in both directions. There is quick recovery from gloom, built through practice of reframing and bolstered by the solid levels of the good stuff. The joy sticks around for longer, built through practice of noticing it and enhanced by reflecting on it.

Chronic WorkGloom

In this example the effects of a gloomy mindset, environment, or situation are evident. The neutral has a hint of gloom and tends to be below the line. Where there are moments of joy, they are low-level and short-lived. They give way to longer, deeper periods of gloom.

Toxic positivity

Here you can see what on the surface looks fantastic – a full week of extreme joy. Of course, these weeks can happen in theory, yet all lives have gloomy parts and denying that can send you into the zone of faking it – outwardly and, even more dangerously, convincing yourself that everything is wonderful!

 Reflection question
- What's the shape of your WorkJoy right now?

 WorkJoy WorkBook
Use the Mapping the Shape of Your WorkJoy template to track your current experience

Developing your WorkJoy mindset

Mindset is the way you think and the beliefs that help you navigate situations. The transition from feeling a bit 'meh' (WorkGloom) to feeling a lot more 'yeah' (WorkJoy) begins with what's going on in your head. There are no magic wands to rid you of the annoyances that are a part of working life. It's an expedition to embark on for yourself as the protagonist of your story. That's not to suggest you should do it alone – in fact the WorkJoy method puts relationships at the heart of the mission (see chapter 7 – **Squads** for more on this).

This adventure to build more joy isn't a one-hit wonder. The magic sits in how you process your thoughts, develop your behaviours, and create helpful habits. It's learning to focus your attention on the things that will make a difference, rather than getting stuck in the quagmire. Over time, this will lead you to better understand how to get more WorkJoy, more often as well as a deep understanding of how to reframe and manage the WorkGloom.

The three Es of WorkJoy

Let's explore the three Es of **Engagement**, **Energy**, and **Experimentation** as approaches to creating and cultivating a more joyful working world for yourself.

Engagement

It's easy to get lost in the world of work and become a passive participant. Maybe you've found yourself stepping back, or checking out at work? Have you stopped putting your hand up for new projects, asking for feedback, or speaking in meetings? Perhaps you've heard yourself moaning yet not taking action to fix the issues you are facing? Sometimes the gradual descent into chronic WorkGloom happens so slowly that you may not notice it until you're stuck in the choppy sea, gasping for some joy, and wondering how it got this bad! Other times a single act has such a big impact that the gloom is acute and painful in an instant.

Did you know that during their career the average person:

- Spends **35%**[3] of their total waking hours working
- Which averages out at just over **13 years**[4] in total
- Or the equivalent of **90,000**[5] hours on the job

These are sobering numbers, especially if those hours are filled with gloom. It's time to stop expecting others to 'fix it' for you and start to take control of your working life. Step into a more joyful mindset by paying attention to what's going on, engaging with your attitude and emotions about work.

Energy

It's not just about noticing what's going on. Being able to write an essay about everything that's not quite right, or defining every moment of WorkGloom to the nth degree, isn't likely to make things better. It is essential that you

[3] K. Thompson, *What percentage of your life will you spend at work?* ReviseSociology. Available from: https://revisesociology.com/2016/08/16/percentage-life-work/ [accessed 11 March 2018].

[4] L. Campbell, *We've broken down your entire life into years spent doing tasks.* HuffPost UK (19 October 2017). Available from: www.huffingtonpost.co.uk/entry/weve-broken-down-your-entire-life-into-years-spent-doing-tasks_n_61087617e4b0999d2084fec5 [accessed 25 August 2022].

[5] D. Buettner, *Finding happiness at work.* Psychology Today (21 February 2011). Available from: www.psychologytoday.com/us/blog/thrive/201102/finding-happiness-work [accessed 25 August 2022].

understand where you get your joy and gloom from. It is also critical to dedicate yourself to action.

It's going to take effort and energy to improve your working life – that's a fact. You're busy – you've got more things on your to-do list than hours in the day to get them done. The idea of adding more items may make you want to go and hide under the duvet! This is where choice comes into the frame.

You can carry on as you are, or you can choose to put some energy into making it better. You can choose to see this as more things on the to-do list, or you can see it as an investment into a brighter future. You can choose to embark on your quest for more joy or you can choose not to take that step. Energy is the biggest catalyst for change. Choice is a powerful thing. Choose wisely!

Experimentation

Experimentation is the key that unlocks the door to more WorkJoy. As the factors that create WorkJoy and WorkGloom are unique to you, so are the solutions to the conundrums you face. There is no single pathway to follow, with items to tick off. There are almost unlimited ways to explore what works for you.

To get into experimenting, be prepared to try new and different things, to break out of old habits and create new ones. Perhaps you may return to some things you've done before that have fallen off your agenda? Maybe you'll head down some avenues that aren't right for you, helping you discover the correct boulevard over time.

Be ready for it to feel awkward and sticky. When that feeling comes, don't step back, or try to circumnavigate it. Walk directly into it, embrace it. That feeling happens just before growth, in the moments before you learn what you really need. Learn to embrace it and one day you may even love it!

Utilizing the three Es

You may find that you're naturally drawn to one of the three Es.

- Perhaps you have a strength in engaging with new things and are keen to learn more about yourself?
- Maybe you're up for investing your energy and have dedicated time to this adventure?
- Are you someone who's all about action and you're eagerly seeking out advice on what to do next?

You may also find that you're unsure about one of the other Es.

- Maybe the idea of being able to find the energy to do this puts you off?
- Or the notion of trying something out of your comfort zone makes you fearful?

You will need to engage all three Es at some point during your quest for more WorkJoy.

Both recognizing your areas of strength and working through those areas that feel slightly daunting will help you to make the most of this toolkit.

 Reflection questions

- Which of the three Es are you drawn to?
- Which of them do you feel less connected to?
- What will you do to get working on all three?

At the end of each chapter, you'll see a summary of ideas on how you can apply the three Es to the topic.

The WorkJoy mindset statements

The WorkJoy mindset can be summarized in these 10 statements:

Engagement	1. I am personally responsible for my levels of joy 2. I stay hopeful even when things are tough 3. I cannot control everything that happens in my work life
Energy	4. I actively seek out joy in the choices I make 5. I focus my attention where it matters most 6. I accept that getting it wrong and failure are part of the process 7. I spread joy to those around me
Experimentation	8. I am in pursuit of progress and not perfection 9. I try new and different things 10. I gather support and help from other people

 Reflection question
- Where are you right now in your beliefs about the WorkJoy mindset statements?

 WorkJoy WorkBook
Head to the WorkBook for the Mindset Tracker template

Your current WorkJoy state

To be able to plan your personal route, it might help to understand where you are right now. Many people are living with a severe case of chronic WorkGloom. In their 2018 survey of 500 employees, A.T. Kearney[6] found that 90% of people expected to feel joy at work, yet only 37% of people felt it. That's a joy gap of 53%. It's terrifying that so many people are seriously unhappy in their working life. Let's take inspiration from this research and work out what your personal joy gap is.

 Reflection questions

- What level of joy are you currently getting? (1 = consistently gloomy and 10 = consistently joyful)
- Now subtract your reality from a 10 (for the purposes of this exercise, this represents a healthy and realistic level of WorkJoy!).
- What's your joy gap?
- How, when, and why does that gap show up for you?
- If you're struggling with a **large joy gap (7+),** you may need to rally the troops to help you get a big dose of WorkJoy ASAP! You'll need to dig deep with the three Es to make a significant change.
- If you've got a **medium joy gap (4–6),** consider which areas are worth focusing your attention on and get experimenting.
- If you've got a **small joy gap (3 or less)**, brilliant – use this toolkit to fine tune, supercharge, and maintain the joy.

Always lead yourself from where you are right now, not the fantasy of where you want to be.

The WorkJoy formulae

There is no prescribed set of steps or 'you must do this' in this toolkit. It's an approach that you can apply to

---

[6] J. Coleman and K. Hedges, *Making joy a priority at work*. Harvard Business Review (17 July 2019). Available from: https://hbr.org/2019/07/making-joy-a-priority-at-work [accessed 20 January 2021].

your thinking and your actions. Essentially, there are two formulae you can use: a passive WorkJoy formula and a more active one. Let's look at each in turn.

Passive WorkJoy formula

WorkJoy = WorkJoy moments – WorkGloom moments

The passive WorkJoy formula is the balance of the joyful moments in your life versus the gloomy moments in any given period, taking note of both the volume and the vigour of each moment:

- *Volume* is the number of times something happens and the regularity.
- *Vigour* is the size and impact of the moment.

When something tiny happens very regularly, it can bring you brilliant amounts of WorkJoy or land you in the pit of WorkGloom. This formula can also mean that one big thing, even if it only happens once, can have the same captivating or crushing impact.

In this passive formula, if you can reduce the gloom and build the joy moments, you will likely feel more WorkJoy. It is a good place to begin to better understand your sources of WorkJoy and WorkGloom – a solid foundation of understanding for you to build upon.

Resource recommendation

To understand your WorkJoy and WorkGloom better, you can take the free 'WorkJoy – Where Do You Get Yours?' experiment at https://createworkjoy.com

Active WorkJoy formula

Once you understand where you get your WorkJoy and WorkGloom from, try this active formula to create greater impact through the choices you make and the actions you take. It focuses on utilizing the Engagement, Energy, and Experimentation approach and applying it with intent in two different directions:

> **WorkJoy = (EEE x cultivating WorkJoy) +**
> **(EEE x reframing WorkGloom)**

If you work with this formula, you are likely to experience transformation in the way you think, feel, and act when working (watch out for the massive impact it will have on your life beyond work too!). At the end of every chapter of this book, I will provide an example of this formula in action, showing you how you could apply the EEE approach to the topics you've just explored to both cultivate WorkJoy and reframe WorkGloom.

Although you do need to pay attention to both ends of the formula, it does not need to be in equal balance. Your brain is naturally drawn to the dark side due to negativity bias.[7] There's good reason for this – it helps protect you and keep you safe from harm. It can also lead to getting lost in your own head, making mountains where molehills once stood, focusing on the worst-case scenario and catastrophizing about the smallest things.

There will always be some gloom that you cannot solve. It takes investment to cultivate WorkJoy, so intentionally

---

[7] H.E. Marano, *Our brain's negative bias.* Psychology Today (revised 9 June 2016). Available from: www.psychologytoday.com/gb/articles/200306/our-brains-negative-bias [accessed 25 August 2022].

place a greater percentage of your Engagement, Energy, and Experimentation on the joyful side. You'll likely find that the gloom seems to reduce in impact as you align to a joyful mindset.

Where you've got to and what's next

Now that you know what WorkJoy is (and isn't!), you have a great foundation to build upon. In this chapter, you worked through:

- How WorkJoy presents itself over time
- The WorkJoy mindset
- The three Es: Engagement, Energy, and Experimentation
- Your current joy gap
- Applying the three Es using the WorkJoy formulae

In the next part of the toolkit, you'll focus your attention on the inner WorkJoy factors, including **Values**, **Boundaries**, **Stories**, and **Learning**. First up is an in-depth look at Life and how work fits in.

PART 2

THE INNER WORKJOY FACTORS

CHAPTER 2

LIFE

Introduction

Now you understand the route to WorkJoy, we're going to park up and talk about life! I've always believed that you can't fix a wonky WorkJoy without looking at what's going on for you outside of work. They go hand in hand, or balloon in balloon, as you'll see in my fabulous exercise (don't skip that one – we'll be coming back to it throughout the book). This chapter is where we'll cover the work you don't get paid to do (like volunteering, caring, etc.) and other – equally vital – things like rest and wellbeing. But first, we need to bust a very big, very annoying myth.

The myth of work/life balance

The notion of work/life balance has been talked about for decades now and if you achieve it, everything will be perfect. Most of us haven't managed to find this utopia. Many people struggling with WorkGloom feel more like a circus performer, juggling with different-sized and weighted objects with sharp corners, whilst riding a unicycle, than they do a calm and collected master balancer.

The very idea of work/life balance makes lots of assumptions. Let's challenge the term, unpick it and, perhaps, find a more realistic way of thinking about how work fits into your life:

- It puts work first in the sentence and there's something powerful about the ordering. Work is an important part of life, yet does it really come first out of everything?

- The phrase ignores the fact that you are still alive when you're working. Your life doesn't stop and start at the office door or Zoom screen. There is much life to be had at work – just think of the experiences, friends, and sense of purpose it gives you.

- It also assumes that things stay static – that the size of work stays the same and that your life outside of work does too. Well, anyone who's worked whilst having a life will tell you that there are times when this simply isn't true:
  - Sometimes life outside of work takes over. Things like building a family, caring for others, having a hobby, or moving house simply fill up all the space (and then some!).
  - Sometimes work takes over. Things like big projects, working towards a qualification, or putting all your effort into achieving a promotion take up bucket loads of time and energy.

The energy you invest trying to find this balance is like trying to find the needle in the haystack of life. It's impossible, and because of this, you feel you've failed, and the self-pity party really gets going. That's not to say that balance isn't a good thing – having anything out of kilter can have a serious impact on your ability to maintain joy. Let's just make sure you're balancing things in a way that makes sense for the real world. Instead of the see-saw of balance, being weighed down at one end or the other, how about we create a more realistic version of what work looks like in the context of life?

The balloons of life

Visualize for a moment a massive transparent balloon (one of those fancy ones from a party shop), that can have other balloons blown up inside it. The transparent balloon is representative of your whole life. Each inner balloon represents a feature of your life that is important to you. One might be friends, another family, one is likely to be work (the paid kind), another could be some of the unpaid work you do, and perhaps you have a few for your favourite hobbies?

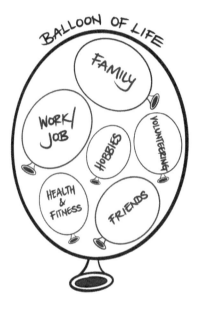

 Reflection question

- Take a few moments to think about which balloons feature in your life and note them down.

The balloons you create in your life will be unique to you. The size of each inner balloon can expand and contract based on the choices you make about how much time and energy you will dedicate to them. Your balloons may also have inner balloons inside of them (for example your work balloon may have your role, the projects you work on, your team, etc. as part of it).

Sometimes, one balloon may need to be larger than all the others, because life throws a variety of wonderful and scary and heart-breaking things at you. That may mean that other balloons need to deflate a little for a while. They're still there, ready and waiting for when you have the space to breathe life into them. You may find that you have too many balloons or some balloons demanding the energy you'd rather invest elsewhere.

The inner balloons are either controllable or at least influenceable (based on your choices). Your outer balloon is fixed by the annoying limitation of time available. You might find that the more you look after the inner balloons, the more the outer balloon feels like it's a little bit more flexible. There are some balloons that act as incredible energy suppliers, giving back to you when you invest in them. These are joyful balloons – keep them, nourish them, love them. Get to know why these balloons give you the joy and consider how you can maximize the impact:

 Reflection questions

- Why does this bring you joy?
- How can you expand the time and energy you give to this?
- What can you learn from this that you could repeat or transfer to another balloon?

You may find that some balloons have been handed to you by someone else. Or some may guzzle up your energy but never offer anything in return. Take some time to analyse these:

Reflection questions

- Why does this bring you gloom?
- How could you rearrange how much space this balloon takes up in your life?
- What would popping this balloon and removing it from your life mean?

The challenge is to allow the balloons to be the right size more often and not allow the single balloon of work to take over all the time.

The space between

Almost as important as the balloons themselves is the space between the balloons. Having 27 fully filled balloons trying to squeeze every breath out of you and filling every second leaves no room for anything else. If your balloons are rubbing up against each other, they're going to create that static that makes your hair stand on end. They will have you headed towards burnout quicker than you can deflate them.

We all need room to do nothing. To experience the joy of having no plans at all. To be in service of nothing and no one for a few minutes, an hour, or even a whole day (parent people – the whole day thing might be a fantasy – perhaps start with space to drink a cuppa whilst it's hot!). Maybe allowing yourself to be bored for once, un-entertained, because being bored is very good for you.[8] Perhaps creating some space to be spontaneous is exactly what you need. An immediate *yes* to an opportunity rather than 'I'm too busy'. Space to add in anything from a quick conversation to a new commitment. Not space for something essential

---

[8] S. Heshmat, *5 benefits of boredom*. Psychology Today (4 April 2020). Available from: www.psychologytoday.com/gb/blog/science-choice/202004/5-benefits-boredom [accessed 25 August 2022].

or necessary. Not space to furnish someone else's need. Something entirely in service of you and yourself.

Be ready to be unashamedly selfish and protect that space. The term selfish is almost always used in the negative, used to describe a character flaw. Language has limited us to putting a binary positive or negative determination on something that is so complex. As the airlines tell us, you need to put your own oxygen mask on first. We need a new word for this kind of selfish. In the meantime, reclaim selfish as a positive and allow the balloons the space to be friction-free, calm, and moveable. Place value on the space between.

Sorting out your balloons

Knowing where to start can be one of the hardest things. It can lead to feeling lost, getting stuck in the dreaded procrastination zone, and taking very little action. Here's one way to get going by quickly sizing up where you want to focus some attention.

 WorkJoy WorkBook

You'll find the Balloon Sorting template in the WorkJoy WorkBook

1. Refer to your balloon of life, thinking what the major balloons (your core elements) in your life are, and write these down (aim for no more than 10 for the purposes of the exercise – so pick the most important).
2. Draw your core life elements into your balloon of life here. Make the size of each balloon represent the combination of the time and energy you currently invest in them – the bigger the amount of time and energy, the bigger the balloon, and vice versa.

3. Give each balloon a score out of 10 (10 = consistent joy and 1 = chronic gloom). Try not to overthink this – it's not a test – base it on your gut feeling. Remember your goal with joy is not 100% joy all the time, so it's normal for some balloons to be lower than others.

4. Then review your current state balloon and consider:
   - Why have you allocated those scores?
   - Which balloons would you like to take up more space?
   - Which balloons would you like to take up less space?
   - What feels out of kilter?
   - What feels about right?
   - What balloons are missing that should be in there?
   - What balloons would you like to pop?

5. Next, think about what size you'd like each balloon to be in the future (remember size is a combination of time and energy) and re-draw your balloon based on this ideal. Obviously, every day will be different, so a snapshot of the average will do – there's always room for adjustment.

6. In your ideal version, write in where you want your score out of 10 to be in six months' time. Be realistic here – if it's currently a 3 and it's a big unwieldy balloon that will require a lot of attention, time, and energy, aiming for a 10 in six months may not be the best idea. For others a 6 out of 10 may be enough (and enough is very important) – so you'll maintain at that level.

7. Pick a balloon to focus on first and define one small action you can take to pay it some attention.

Once you've completed this exercise, you'll have a good understanding of what's important to you, which areas are on the joy track, which have gone off-piste, and where you might want to focus your attention.

Unpaid work

The reality of modern life is that in addition to your paid work, most people also have unpaid work they need or want to do.

Responsibilities

At one end of the spectrum, there is work that is related to your life responsibilities. For many people, that includes caring for others. From the estimated 13 million working parents with school age children,[9] to the one in eight people who provide unpaid care to their families and friends in the UK,[10] a huge proportion of people work beyond their paid employment. Unpaid care and domestic work have an estimated value of between 10% and 39% of a country's GDP.[11] Just because it's unpaid does not mean it isn't valuable. It is work and it can bring you as much joy and gloom as (or more of it than) the paid kind.

Simply being an adult means there's life admin and daily chores to contend with. From paying bills, to walking the dog, to cleaning, cooking, gardening... the list is endless, and the mental load is high. Some of these things may bring you joy, some may be neutral, and some may be sources of gloom. Because more than one thing can be true at the same time, some may be a combination of both. Responsibilities come with expectations and millennia of conditioning of what you should and shouldn't be doing (including gender-based roles). It often tugs on your heartstrings and is likely to

---

[9] *Concern about future from UK working parents linked to final restrictions lifting.* Working Families (17 June 2021). Available from: https://workingfamilies. org.uk/news/flextheuk2021/ [accessed 25 August 2022].

[10] *Facts & figures.* Carers UK. Available from: www.carersuk.org/ news-and-campaigns/press-releases/facts-and-figures [accessed 25 August 2022].

[11] *Redistribute unpaid work.* UN Women. Available from: www. unwomen.org/en/news/in-focus/csw61/redistribute-unpaid-work [accessed 25 August 2022].

be present at the best and worst of times. It's almost always deeply entangled with who you are and how you see yourself.

Volunteering

At the other end of the unpaid work spectrum is volunteering, which nearly 33% of the UK population took part in during 2019.[12] When people choose to invest their time and energy in activities that are meaningful to them, they often find the joy. This can be through the work itself, from the notion of giving back, or by supporting a cause close to their hearts. The communities built up around volunteering give connection to new and different networks. It's no wonder volunteering has been found to have significant mental health benefits.[13] If you've never tried out volunteering, it may well be an interesting experiment to explore and discover what joys it can bring.

A word on wellbeing

This book isn't about wellbeing (there are thousands of resources for this topic) yet getting more WorkJoy will have an impact on how you feel. If you want the energy to fill up your non-work-related balloons, you need to take care of your wellbeing. You will know best what works for you as it's a deeply personal topic. If you're seeking some inspiration of small things you can do with little time and no cost, here are some ideas. Simply pick one to start with and do it consistently. Then, when it feels like a natural part of your day, pick another one. The build over time will be manageable and the impact could be enormous.

---

[12] S. Lock, *Share of adults volunteering in England 2005–2020*. Statista (28 October 2021). Available from: www.statista.com/statistics/419987/ volunteers-engagement-uk-england/ [accessed 25 August 2022].

[13] *Volunteering may help you live longer*. Age UK (23 August 2013). Available from: www.ageuk.org.uk/latest-news/archive/volunteering-may-help-you-live-longer/ [accessed 25 August 2022].

The key here is building and maintaining the habits (for further advice on how to do this see chapter 11 – **Goals**).

Fifteen little ways to look after yourself

Get yourself outside	• Go for a 10-minute walk around the block/your workplace • Have your morning coffee/tea outside and watch the world go by • Do a walk-and-talk meeting (in person or on the phone)
Take brain breaks	• Reclaim your lunch break away from your desk/workspace • Listen to a podcast/watch a TED talk/read a chapter of a book • Complete a guided meditation or mindfulness session
Move your body	• Put on your favourite tune and take a three-minute dance break • Take part in an activity that makes you smile (or try out some new ones) • Stand up from your desk (if you work at one) at least once an hour
Nourish your body	• Drink water – by the time you're thirsty you're already dehydrated[14] • Eat food (who hasn't skipped lunch to meet a deadline?) • Eat carbs – your brain needs them to function[15] (not just biscuits though – I checked)

---

[14] D. Benson, *Thirsty? You're already dehydrated*. Baylor College of Medicine (9 August 2021). Available from: www.bcm.edu/news/thirsty-you-are-already-dehydrated [accessed 25 August 2022].

[15] B. Stallwood with S. Mather, *Psychological safety*. WorkJoy Jam (series 3, episode 4, 11 October 2021) [podcast]. Available from: https://anchor.fm/workjoyjam/episodes/S3-E4---Sam-Mather---Pyschological-Safety-e189iij [accessed 25 August 2022].

Sleep	• Have a screen time curfew before bed • Go to bed earlier[16] • Take a nap if you're tired[17]

And one final one for good measure – plan in and take *all* of the annual leave/paid time off you are offered.

 WorkJoy story – Time for living

I'd moved to London for my job and was working 14-hour days. I didn't have the time or the energy after work to find myself a group of friends who lived locally, so I started to feel isolated. My life and work were so out of balance and I identified that what I wanted to work on was building a social life outside of work. It turned out to be a really important step as I left my job shortly after the move.

The WorkJoy toolkit helped me to weigh up whether work/ life balance actually exists and prompted me to explore what I wanted to do with my free time. I'd started working from home and saw how important it was to get out during the day. I also set aside time to exercise and switch off from my screen. I started reading books again! The irony is that I now get so much joy from my work that I don't mind working in the evenings.

The big lesson for me is that things will shift. It's not always an equal amount of work and life and that's okay. What's important is that now I know when I need to get my balance back and how to do that.

---

[16] R. Osmun, *9 science-backed reasons why you should go to bed early*. HuffPost (1 May 2015). Available from: www.huffpost.com/entry/go-to-bed-early_b_7157026 [accessed 25 August 2022].
[17] *The benefits of napping*. Harvard Health (8 May 2012). Available from: www.health.harvard.edu/healthbeat/the-benefits-of-napping [accessed 25 August 2022].

The route to WorkJoy – Life

Using the active WorkJoy formula, let's consider some ideas of how you could use the three Es of Engagement, Energy, and Experimentation within the context of **Life** to both cultivate WorkJoy and reframe WorkGloom.

Life	Cultivating WorkJoy	Reframing WorkGloom
Engagement	Direct your thinking towards work being a part of that bigger thing called life rather than attempting to create work/life 'balance'.	If you've got stuck with a work balloon that's squishing your other balloons out of shape (or even popping them), reframe your thinking towards what's in your control and focus there.
Energy	Invest your energy in defining the things that are most important in your life using the **balloons of life** activity and use this thinking to guide the choices you make.	Consider whether any balloons may need to deflate a little to create space for the things that matter most to you and remember it's ok to be selfish!
Experimentation	Experiment with the simple and easy **wellbeing** experiments. You'll be amazed how looking after yourself can contribute to your WorkJoy.	Pick a balloon that is contributing to your gloom and dig deep into the who, what, and why – and then do something about it!

Now that you've explored your **Life** and what's important to you, let's connect with your **Values** (chapter 3) and how they can guide your thinking and your actions.

CHAPTER 3

VALUES

Introduction

From lifestyle blogs to business boardrooms, values are often talked about, yet rarely do I see people squeezing every drop of juice from them. I know that values can sound like one of those buzz words, but I promise that working with your values could be a critical piece of your WorkJoy puzzle. You'll likely find that some of the gloom you experience is when your values are not aligned to your situation. In this chapter, we'll cover what values are, the link to behaviours, and how your values interact with other people's. To start with, let's define what values really are.

Personal values

The dictionary definition of values goes something like this: 'the principles that help you to decide what is right and wrong, and how to act in various situations'.[18] The challenge with this definition is the idea that right and wrong are binary. In real life there's a massive array of complex, situational aspects to consider. Two people could both hold a value deeply, yet the line they draw between what feels good and what feels bad could be miles apart. Then how values are expressed in terms of what is said and done (the behaviours) could vary in many directions. Perhaps we can

---

[18] *Values*. Cambridge Dictionary. Available from: https://dictionary.cambridge.org/dictionary/english/values [accessed 7 September 2022].

expand the thinking to how they sit with your principles and influence your behaviours:

Values: Values are deeply linked to your emotions – they are heart led. They are the things that you care about in your life. They help you make choices and decisions that feel right for you.

Principles: Principles are linked to your beliefs about what is the 'right' way to do things – they are thought led and influenced by your background (family, culture, environment, etc.). They act as your internal moral compass.

Behaviours: Behaviours are how you show up in the world – they are action led. In theory, they are the way in which you demonstrate your values and principles through what you say and what you do.

Sometimes the behaviours you demonstrate make it obvious what your values and principles are. When you're behaving in a way that aligns, it can feel that all is right in the world. At other times, your behaviours won't match what you care about. Those awkward moments when you've lost your rag (even though one of your values is kindness), felt compelled to stay quiet (when you'd say speaking up for others is important), or adapted your position for the sake of ease, or fear, or because you simply can't be bothered (when you would say being truthful is a value).

When you know your values and are (mostly) living and behaving in alignment, you may feel a sense of security, certainty, and reassurance. They also act as an anchor point when things feel difficult, guiding you through tough times, helping you weigh up options, set **Boundaries** (as we'll cover in chapter 4), and make choices. When you go off-piste from your values, it can feel that things aren't quite right, like you're in the quick-sand and unable to find your footing. It becomes difficult to find your direction and make the right decisions.

The idea that if you can stand by your values 100% of the time you'll be happier is a noble one, yet it is almost impossible to achieve:

- Sometimes you'll make choices that don't align with your values.
- Sometimes your values rub up against each other, causing friction, and you must choose one at the cost of sacrificing the other.
- Sometimes you don't even consider your values and, instead, go along with a plan without a second thought – in pursuit of peace, or because you simply act on what you want in the moment.

In addition, your values are constantly interacting with other people's values.

Other people's values, principles, and behaviours

When you observe behaviours in others, it's easy to make assumptions about what values they hold. You are not a mind reader, so you take clues from what happens on the outside. If you've ever heard yourself mumbling phrases like 'they clearly don't care about…', then you have fallen into that trap. Unless you know someone well, have spent time with them in many, varied situations (the good, the bad, and the ugly) and have had those deep conversations about values and principles, you're unlikely to be able to define what that someone cares about. Withhold your judgement – you never really know what's going on in another person's life.

Organizational values

Many organizations have defined values, describing the 'way we do things around here'. They can be based in the reality, or they can be aspirational, setting the tone for how it could be. Whether they are outward-facing values that align with the business brand or are inward, employee-facing values that align with the employer brand (or a combination of both), the values an organization subscribes to will inevitably have an impact on you. Even if there are no shiny values etched on the wall, the organization will likely have values in some way. You might describe them as the culture of the organization, or the way people treat each other. Organizational values are statements of intent. You may interpret what they mean through your own lens, relating them to your own thinking and experiences. Every other person in the organization will do the same thing. Whether that's 10 slightly different perspectives, or 10,000 alternative views, organizational values are complex because they are not controllable.

 WorkJoy story – Aligning your values

I really believe that 'values' has become an overused word. Companies can say their values are whatever they like, but the culture is organic. It never lies. I was working for a business, on the operations side. They'd paid for me to do my Chartered Institute for Personnel and Development (CIPD) human resources (HR) training, and I'd worked really hard on the company values. I was an obvious fit for an HR role when one came up, but they brought someone else in to do it.

The toolkit encouraged me to truly think about how I could cultivate WorkJoy if I didn't value and appreciate the organization I was working for, and they didn't value and appreciate me. I'm a people pleaser so for a while I just got on with the work, but from the moment I worked out my values, there was no going back. It became really important for me to work for a company I can be completely myself with. I realized that I was never going to get joy there and, in the end, I left.

Finding a company that I aligned with became a big thing. I wasn't sure how to go about it, but I always stuck to my values. I actually made two moves to get closer to what I wanted, but the WorkJoy tools gave me courage. I reached out to someone whose values aligned with mine and they created a position within their organization for me, three days a week. They've really got it sussed. I'm a strong part of the team and I'm really happy there. The other two days a week I work for myself, and I get to choose clients whose values I align with as well. It's phenomenal the difference it's made.

Now I encourage others to cultivate their own WorkJoy. It isn't just handed to you on a plate and it's not just down to the business. It's down to believing in yourself and challenging yourself. You only live once.

Defining your personal values

You already have some idea of what's important to you. Whether you'd describe this as values is another matter. There are many books and processes out there for working out what values are important to you, but here are four experiments that might help. Feel free to seek out other ones that go deeper than this chapter can!

 WorkJoy WorkBook

You will find the Values Exploration template in the WorkJoy WorkBook

Opposites	Reverse engineering
• Ask yourself the question 'what behaviours do I dislike in others?' • Write a list of those behaviours • Consider the opposite of those behaviours • Theme the behaviours together • Give each theme a word that best describes it • Build from there	• Ask yourself the question 'what behaviours do I display when I'm at my very best?' • Write a list of those behaviours • Switch them from behaviours into values words • Give each theme a word that best describes it • Build from there
Free writing	**Crowd source**
• Ask yourself the question 'what is important to me in my life? What do I really care about?' • Set a timer for six minutes • Start writing, do not stop, do not overthink, just keep writing • Once the six minutes are completed, review your thinking, and pick out the main themes • Give each theme a word that best describes it • Build from there	• Select three to five people whom you trust and admire and who know you well (choose people from different areas of your life to get good range) • Ask them to describe you when you're at your best • Consider how their feedback relates to your behaviours • Theme the behaviours together • Give each theme a word that best describes it • Build from there

Check and challenge

Once you've created a list of three to five words that describe your values, dig a little deeper, and test them out.

Reflection questions

- How do these words make you feel?
- How would you describe what they mean to other people?
- Would you be proud if other people described you using these words?
- What behaviours would you need to display to make these values clear to others?
- How often are you living up to these values?
- When you're not behaving in line with them, what's going on in your world?

Living your values: The values equalizer

Much like when they conflict with other people's values, your own values can cause friction when in competition with each other, causing that ache of internal conflict. Like anything in life, values apply only within the unique context of a situation, an environment, or a moment in time. Rigidity will not help you here. Back in the day, before music was on-demand on a phone, people had hi-fis. These machines had something on them called a graphic equalizer. You may remember these, or you may be thinking 'what on earth are you talking about?'. Feel free to google this now so that you can get into the analogy! A graphic equalizer takes the elements of music and dials some up and dials some down depending on what is the best mix for that moment.

In any situation, you may need to dial up one of your values and dial down another, deciding what is contextually appropriate. Perhaps one of the values isn't relevant to what's going on, perhaps another isn't helpful and could cause more issues than it solves. This doesn't mean you aren't fully living your values.

It means you're being savvy about how to apply them. An example might be:

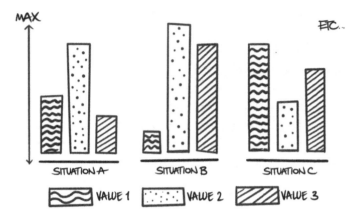

- You hold a value about transparency because you value open and clear communications.
- You also hold the value of trust deeply because it's the foundation of great relationships.
- If a colleague tells you something in confidence, you'll need to choose which gets a higher weighting.
- In this circumstance you'll likely pick the trust (possibly without even consciously considering it). This doesn't mean you're not being transparent; you're carefully choosing the right things to be transparent about.

The key to keeping it joyful is to know what your minimum standard is and not to go below that line.

Connecting personal and organizational purpose, values, and principles

There is a lot to be said for finding work where your personal and the organizational values align. If you've got kindness, creativity, and learning on your list and the organization you work for, or want to work for, espouses those too, you may be going 'tick – this is going to be awesome'! There may also be times when your personal values are misaligned to an organization – for example if you value humility, but the only way to get noticed in your organization is to be boastful.

An organization's values are only as solid as the behaviours of the people who work there, and their interpretations of the organizational values will mingle amongst their personal values. Their behaviours will be a combination of these, so they'll also be imperfect and inconsistent. Some organizations have values that you can touch and feel as soon as you're working with them. The behaviours align with the words, and it all feels authentic. In others the behaviours are so contradictory to the values, you wonder who on earth created them. There are multiple directions and combinations, including:

- Great sounding values + great behaviours (fabulous – where do I sign?)
- Great sounding values + awful behaviours (inauthentic)
- Awful sounding values (or no stated values) + great behaviours (identity crisis)
- Awful sounding values (or no stated values) + awful behaviours (run for the hills)

 Reflection questions

- What values do your organization promote (if any)?
- How do those values align with the behaviours you observe?

The link between values and purpose

Let's look at how values and purpose are linked to each other.

Personal purpose

Finding your purpose is a quest that many people embark on, hoping it will be the magic wand that leads to a wonderful life. There is research to suggest that people who have a sense of purpose are happier (and live longer) than those that don't,[19] making it a worthy WorkJoy topic! At the newsworthy end are those who are attempting to change the world, with stories of massive goals – like exploring space (Elon Musk) or saving the planet (Leonardo DiCaprio). The grandiose nature of these stories involving wealthy individuals can be off-putting when it comes to uncovering your own purpose. Let's change the narrative and remember that your personal purpose does not need to be grand, bold, or even particularly innovative.

The power of multi- and micro-purposes

Your purpose also doesn't have to be singular. You may have a bigger purpose to connect to and then set a daily intention. You can have multiple purposes. You may even have different purposes for different things. A more life-based purpose and a more work-based purpose, perhaps? It could be a theme that guides how you invest your energy.[20] This approach helps to avoid being pulled in multiple

---

[19] M.J. Barkan, *Why it's important to find your purpose in life (with 3 helpful tips)*. Tracking Happiness (3 July 2022). Available from: www.trackinghappiness.com/important-to-have-purpose-in-life/ [accessed 7 September 2022].

[20] C.G.P. Grey, *Your theme*. YouTube (CGP Grey channel) (26 January 2020). Available from: www.youtube.com/watch?v=NVGuFdX5guE [accessed 7 September 2022].

directions. It's also something that can adapt with you over the course of your life.

It would be neat and tidy if you decided your purpose when you were in your twenties and fresh into the world of work and you simply kept on swimming down that lane. Real life changes how you feel about things – some elements will move up your list of importance and others will move down. New things get added and others are lost through time. Your experiences will continue to teach you what's important and, more importantly, the compelling reason as to why. Your purpose, or purposes, can evolve with you.

How to find alignment with your organization

Rather than focus on the values themselves, realign your attention to the behaviours of the people around you:

Look to the leadership

- What behaviours do they display?
- What's the role model archetype around here?
- Do they demonstrate behaviours you can respect 70%–80% of the time?

Consider your colleagues

- What do your teammates and close colleagues offer in their behaviours?
- Are they with you, do they support you? Have they got your back?
- Could you rely on them in a crisis? Do they care about you personally?

Delight in diversity

- A team, an organization, that all has the exact same values, the same thinking, may sound like a lovely, conflict-free place to be. In fact, it's likely to be devoid of creativity, seriously lacking in inspiration, and more likely to fail in its tasks than one with greater levels of cognitive diversity.
- Understanding and valuing different perspectives can be the key to a high-performing team.[21]

Seek out a working environment where your values are complemented by the people you are surrounded by, where the sum of the value of your combined behaviours is greater than yours are alone. Where you can be yourself and others can be true to themselves. Where you can all get on board with the company's purpose, mission, and values, and use your personal style and perspective to add value and get value in equal measure.

 Reflection questions

- Are you able to live your values at work?
- Do your values align with (some) of the organizational values?
- Where are the misalignments (if any)?

The route to WorkJoy – Values

Using the active WorkJoy formula, let's consider some ideas of how you could use the three Es of Engagement, Energy, and Experimentation within the context of **Values** to both cultivate WorkJoy and reframe WorkGloom.

---

[21] M. Syed, *Rebel ideas: The power of diverse thinking* (2021).

Values	Cultivating WorkJoy	Reframing WorkGloom
Engagement	Engage with the idea of themes or micro-purposes for your work-related projects. For example, on Project A my theme is all about collaboration, and on Project B I'm turning my humility value down so I can promote my team's work.	Direct your thinking towards how your values align with other people's. You might be surprised how just one shared approach can build a more positive relationship.
Energy	Invest your energy in defining how your personal values apply in your professional setting. Which ones are most important to you at work? How do these show up in your behaviours? (It's okay that some may be better suited to your life outside of work.)	Consider the behaviours that feel most natural and joyful to you and assess these against what you demonstrate at work. Are you missing opportunities to be yourself or is your style out of kilter?
Experimentation	Experiment with the values equalizer to understand where, when, and with whom you will adjust your dials (and where you draw the line of your 'minimum standard').	Avoid making snap judgements about what people care about by getting to know them better, especially those you find harder to connect with (see chapter 7).

Now that you've explored your **Values**, let's figure out how creating the right **Boundaries** (chapter 4) can help you cultivate more WorkJoy.

BOUNDARIES

Introduction

Following the exploration of your life and your values, let's dive in and consider your boundaries. Those wonderful fences that enable you to spend your time doing the joyful things. On the surface, they can seem quite simple, yet working them out and applying them can feel complicated. One thing I know for sure is that a lack of boundaries, especially with your time, is a sure-fire way to gloom! When I've had my people-pleaser hat on and not been clear on my boundaries, I've ended up depleted of energy. In this chapter, you'll cover the challenges of limited time and a model that will help you consider different types of boundaries. Let's step back first and look at how the boundaries between work and life have moved.

The blurring of boundaries

The separation between work and home life has been disappearing since the dawn of the digital era. The old structure of 9am to 5pm, seated at a desk, in a specific location, is no longer the standard for office-based workers. For more than a decade, access to work beyond a determined time and place, as well as globalization, has meant that the work day has expanded and extended. There's also a huge population of people who work in industries such as healthcare and hospitality who work shift patterns as standard and there are also many roles that cannot be done from home. You may have found that the 'always on' culture has invaded your life. The onslaught of Covid-19 led to mass working from home for the first time. It was a forced experiment in fundamentally changing the way we approach work, followed by many organizations initiating a 'hybrid' approach. In fact, 78% of organizations surveyed in the UK[22] are now offering employees the option to work a proportion of their time remotely. In many ways this unplanned experiment is a huge success – a change for the better, with greater flexibility being one of the positive outcomes. To begin with, the sense of shared challenge and the excitement of the new world order had people espousing home working. 'I've got an extra three hours a day because I'm working from home' and 'it's so easy to do our meetings online, I don't know why we didn't already do this' was the shared song sheet.

As time went on, the other side of the coin revealed itself. Those extra three hours had stopped being used for morning walks and Zoom quizzes. The initial digital-meeting joy had turned into the gloom of Zoom fatigue[23] and people were craving real, human connection. More than one thing can be true at the same time:

- For every hour saved in commuting time, it feels like two hours of extra work are added.
- For every 'this flexibility makes us more inclusive', there's someone else struggling to feel connected.

---

[22] *Three-quarters of employers now offer hybrid working but employers are split over whether it will last*. CIPD (27 June 2022). Available from: www.cipd.co.uk/about/media/press/270622-cipd-hybrid-working-splits-employers#gref [accessed 7 September 2022].
[23] L. Fosslien and M.W. Duffy, *How to combat Zoom fatigue*. Harvard Business Review (29 April 2020). Available from: https://hbr.org/2020/04/how-to-combat-zoom-fatigue [accessed 12 April 2022].

- For every 'we'll be managing on outputs and not time in the office', there's someone missing out on a career-enhancing opportunity because they weren't in the room.

The situation lived out during a global pandemic is nowhere near normal. The lack of connection was felt beyond work. This great experiment on how to make the hybrid approach work is going to be a feature of working life over the coming years. However this story plays out, one thing is for sure – the boundaries that once existed between work and home life have been well and truly broken down. The disappearing boundaries are a source of WorkGloom for many people, yet this truth is often disguised under the phrases 'I have too much to do', 'I am overwhelmed', or 'I wish I had more time'.

The issue with time

There are always just 24 hours in a day, 7 days in a week, and 365 days in a year, yet many people experience a weird relationship with time. Different people have varying responsibilities and pulls on their time and it's important to recognize that time outside of work is a privilege not every person has access to.

You can get lost in the flow of a project, or binge watch the latest TV series, and time seems to whizz by in an instant when you're with friends. You may also find yourself counting the seconds until the meeting is over, or waiting for the day to end, and that email reply you've been painstakingly crafting feels like weeks for just two lines of text. Time seems to slow down – and not in a wonderful standing-on-a-beach-taking-in-sea-air way, but in the crushing 'what am I doing here?' gloomy kind of way.

This pendulum swing between flow[24] and wishing your time away means you experience time differently depending on the situation. When you add on extended working days and an increasingly full life, some people have taken to staying up late after all the day's work is complete – a phenomenon being called 'revenge bedtime procrastination'.[25] It comes at the expense of sleep, which can cause major physical and mental issues – including a weakened immune system and inability to process information,[26] let alone the impact it will have on your levels of joy. It's almost impossible to feel anything more than neutral when you're tired.

It is likely that you'll experience the feeling of time poverty at some point and research shows that those who feel time-poor experience less joy in their life.[27] This research also suggests that we 'overestimate the amount of time needed to enjoy an experience' – yet even a few minutes is enough to build some joy in to your life. It is so ingrained that life being full is normal that often the response to the question 'how is it going?' is simply 'busy'.

The same research suggests that the happiest people use their money to buy time. As this statement is filled with privilege, let's not spend time working on this one. If you can invest in other people to support you, it may be worth seeing what you can outsource. If it's not something you can do (or do yet), the rest of this book will consider what

[24] *What is a flow state and what are its benefits?* Headspace. Available from: www.headspace.com/articles/flow-state [accessed 7 September 2022].

[25] K. Cherry, *What is revenge bedtime procrastination?* Verywell Mind (6 October 2021). Available from: www.verywellmind.com/what-is-revenge-bedtime-procrastination-5189591 [accessed 7 September 2022].

[26] M. Walker, *Why we sleep: The new science of sleep and dreams* (2018).

[27] A. Whillans, *Time for happiness.* Harvard Business Review (24 January 2019). Available from: https://hbr.org/2019/01/time-for-happiness [accessed 19 April 2021].

you can do without financial investment, because although you cannot create more hours in the day, you can learn how to use your time more joyfully by creating boundaries that protect your space.

The challenge with boundaries

Boundaries can make or break your mood, setting you up for success when they fit or leading you down a pathway of gloom if they are misshapen. You're going to focus on time-related boundaries in this toolkit, yet the same theory can be applied to different types. The challenges people often find with creating, implementing, and maintaining boundaries often fall into four categories:

1. **They are too strict, and this has a negative impact on the people around you.**
   If boundaries are too strict or the wrong things have too strict a boundary, you may fall into the trap of becoming a person who is difficult to live or work with. You've met those people who are so inflexible that they become a drain on you!

2. **They are too flexible and don't really act as boundaries at all.**
   If you set boundaries, but move them at the whim of others, you are in danger of pleasing everyone else and making your own life miserable. A boundary that is rarely upheld isn't a boundary at all – you're giving everyone permission to encroach on your precious time.

3. **They are someone else's boundaries and not your own.**
   When you're on a mission to change, develop, or grow, you may seek out inspiration from others. Trying to

copy and paste someone else's hard-earned work into your own life is likely to be a mis-fit for you.

4. **They are out of date.**
   As time moves on, your priorities and requirements will change. Boundaries that once worked well for you may no longer be hitting the mark as they once did. As you evolve over time, so must your boundaries.

Defining your boundaries

When it comes to managing limited time, your boundaries will enable you to make choices that work for you. Allocating your boundaries into one of these categories could assist you in knowing when to stand firm and when to let things go.

- **Non-negotiables** – the boundaries you hold firmly
- **Bouncy boundaries** – the boundaries that adapt depending on the situation
- **Free-flex** – the boundaries that are the most adaptable

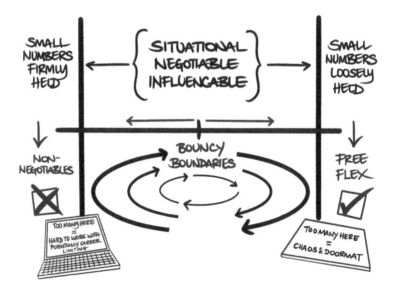

Working out your boundaries

In this diagram, you'll see how the three types of boundaries work. Working from the firmly held non-negotiables, through the more nuanced bouncy boundaries that are applied based on the situation and on to the free-flex option. Keep reading to discover what your unique boundaries are by working through this experiment.

 WorkJoy WorkBook

The Boundaries template can be found in the WorkJoy WorkBook

Before you embark on the experiment, recall an area of your working life where you want to have clearly defined boundaries. Keep this in mind when working through each step.

Your non-negotiable boundaries

It's likely you'll need a few critically important, firmly held boundaries. Too many and you may become too rigid, too few and your time might be eaten by someone else.

Why: Compelling reason	Define the compelling reason for you wanting to put a boundary in place – connect with this why as well as the what and the how. This is likely to be connected to your personal **Values** (see chapter 3).
What: The boundary I will hold firm	Define what the boundary looks like and sounds like – being as specific as possible. This could include creating language about how you will communicate this boundary to other people.

How: Making it happen	Consider how you will implement and maintain this boundary. What changes need to happen to make it a reality? Who needs to be involved? How will you check in and make sure it's working?
Breaking it: The *only* times I will allow the boundary to be broken	Even with non-negotiable boundaries, there may be the exception that proves the rule. Use some situations you've found challenging before to assess the difference between a genuine exception and just flexing too far.

Your bouncy boundaries

It's not always going to be a X = yes or Y = no as there are many factors involved and trying to oversimplify can make it more challenging in the long run. There will be different reasons for saying yes or no, for different situations, times, and people. Bouncy boundaries are the antidote to saying yes and becoming overwhelmed and saying no and getting a reputation for being unhelpful.

Situational	Many boundaries cannot be predefined as they're nuanced. It may be about weighing up the pros and cons, making a best guess in the moment. It can be helpful to pause and understand where the situation fits into your personal priorities and values before deciding.
Conditional	This may help when you're prepared to do something for a certain person, or in a specific situation, but only if there's a quid-pro-quo arrangement. Understand what you are prepared to negotiate. It's the 'if I do X, I'll need Y in return' or 'I can do that, but which of the other actives on my list should we deprioritize to make this happen' or even an 'I will make it happen this time, but this cannot happen again' conversation.
Personal	There are some people in your life who will probably nearly always get a yes. Define who these people are up front – it will make it easier to draw the line when you need to. Consider people who are important and those who can make or break your day. The ones who always support you. For these people, a firmly held boundary may be thrown out of the window if they need you.

Your free-flex boundaries

It's also helpful to have some situations and some people where the boundaries are much more flexible. In her book *Year of yes*,[28] Shonda Rhimes challenged herself to start saying *yes* to more things. To create the space to have fun and to try new things. You only need a few situations and a very limited number of people in this category. Too many and you're in danger of overcommitting and, potentially, being taken advantage of! Consider these two questions to work out where your free-flex boundaries may come into play:

---

[28] S. Rhimes, *Year of yes: How to dance it out, stand in the sun and be your own person* (2016).

What	Who
What opportunities would you make your best efforts to say *yes* to whenever it's possible to do so?	Who are the people you would move mountains for, cancel other plans for, and make sure you're there for when they need you?
Examples could be:	Examples could be:
• **Work-related** – a career-enhancing opportunity, the chance to learn something new, or even a conversation with an interesting person • **Life-related** – having fun doing something that is pure joy (hobbies, sports, going out for dinner – whatever floats your joy boat)	• **Work-related** – a brilliant boss / mentor who is dedicated to developing your career always getting a yes (as opposed to a terrible boss who takes advantage needing stronger boundaries!) • **Life-related** – key people (see chapter 7 – **Squads**) for whom you are there, whatever they need of you and whenever they need you

WorkJoy story – Respecting yourself through boundaries

I'd been working as a marketing coordinator for just under three years and felt really stuck in it. Not long after I started the role, we had numerous leadership changes and a high staff turnover, so work became all about firefighting. It was also up to me to train new starters whilst balancing an incredibly unfulfilling workload. This shouldn't have been my responsibility but I'm a self-proclaimed overachiever – I felt like I should have been able to do it all. I wasn't achieving anything, but I didn't have the clarity to go to my

manager and say, 'Look, this isn't my fault. I need support.'
By the time the pandemic hit, I was completely depleted –
creatively, professionally, and personally. My relationships
were suffering, and I was on the verge of burnout.

Before furlough, I had been working 7am–7pm so the break
and working from home really gave me space to think. Using
the WorkJoy toolkit I asked myself some tough questions:
What do I want to do? And where does it all fit in? I saw
that, yes, my personality had driven me to give 110% but
my company was making me feel like I was still not meeting
what my role required of me. I hadn't set any boundaries,
and they had completely taken advantage of that. Joining
the WorkJoy community, I met others in a similar position
and finally realized, 'It's not just me!' As it turns out, I'm
actually really good at what I do! When furlough ended,
I didn't want to return to work and WorkJoy gave me the
courage to start applying for new jobs and to seek a change.

I started a new role as a Communications Business Partner
at a not-for-profit, with a much better understanding of
what my boundaries would be, and how to live a life outside
of work. Then a freelance opportunity came along, and I
had the capacity and the self-knowledge to take that too.
Alongside my 9–5 and my freelancing, I have a passion for
wellbeing and run my own affiliate marketing business. I
probably work the same hours or even more than I used
to, but I love it. I don't have to give absolutely everything
to my day job because I'm performing above par, and I
no longer have to choose what to drop. Finally, I can take
time off properly and say, 'I'm going to be holidaying up
a mountain and I won't have WIFI', and I'll only do the
things I enjoy doing during that time. Boundaries are
absolutely fundamental to making it all work. At the end of
the day, it's about having respect for myself.

Implementing boundaries

The next challenge is to go from knowing what you want your boundaries to look like, to implementing them. It's about making choices on what you will invest your time into and who you will spend it with. In many situations, the answer may be obvious, you'll have that gut feel that says a big *yes* or a definite *no*. When you're not sure, trying out these three stages may help you work through each situation.

Pause

You may want to please other people and think you need to decide immediately. Sometimes this may be true, yet in many cases, this pressure comes from within! The first step to implementing better boundaries is to simply pause. The pause could be quick whilst you mentally tot up the score. You may need to take more time to properly consider and discuss the issue before returning with an answer. Some phrases that might help you politely pause are:

- 'What an offer! Can I get back to you tomorrow with an answer?'
- 'I need to weigh up how much time I can commit to this with my other priorities, let me look at my diary and get back to you…'
- 'I'm really honoured you thought of me… let me check if I can fully commit as I would want to be all in on this one.'

Ponder

When considering your options, you may benefit from looking at either end of the yes/no spectrum, analysing where they fit with your non-negotiable, bouncy, or free-flex boundaries and what each of those options would mean. Ask yourself:

If I say *yes*:

- What might I gain/learn/get from this experience?
- What joy might come with this? What gloom could I envisage?
- What might I need to say *no* to to allow space for it in my life?
- What am I prepared to give or sacrifice to make it happen?

If I say *no*:

- What might I miss out on?
- What joy might come with saying no? What gloom could I envisage?
- What might I be able to say *yes* to if I don't take this on?
- What am I not prepared to give or sacrifice for this?

Be mindful of the difference between missing out on a great opportunity and simply saying yes through the fear of missing out (FOMO is a serious boundary crusher!). You may have a clear answer after you've worked through the questions. For trickier decisions, you may want to engage in conversation to help you decide. Perhaps that's a necessary conversation in certain circumstances (e.g., for opportunities that may impact on other people) and at other times it may be helpful to get some outside perspective.

Pick

You will need to make a choice and that choice may not be as binary as yes or no. It could be yes with caveats, or yes but not now. It could be a direct no or just a not yet. Saying no is an activity that many people find challenging.[29] That's why so

---

[29] F.D. Barth, *Why is it hard to say 'no' and how can you get better at it?* Psychology Today (15 January 2016). Available from: www. psychologytoday.com/gb/blog/the-couch/201601/why-is-it-hard-say-no-and-how-can-you-get-better-it [accessed 7 September 2022].

many people find themselves overcommitted. There are many reasons why *no* feels difficult. From wanting to please people, to not wanting to let people down, to FOMO, the reasons to say *yes* when you want to say *no* can feel compelling!

Here are some different ways you can say *no* or *yes*.

Saying *no* when you want to say *no*

The trick with a well-delivered *no* is to be clear and concise. There's a tendency to apologize and make excuses, to tell people all the reasons why you can't do it. Perhaps something like this might be less waffly:

- 'It's going to be a *no* from me as I'm focusing on other priorities right now.'
- 'Thank you for the kind offer, it's not something I can commit to right now.'
- 'Although I'm grateful for the offer, this one's not where my passion lies.'

Saying *no* when you want to say *yes*

You've made the choice to say *no* for good reason. You've worked through the steps and made your decision, now you need to communicate it and stick by it. You could try a message like the below and leave it open for the future:

- 'I would love to, yet I simply don't have the time.'
- 'If there's another opportunity in the future, I would love to say yes then.'

You could even use this as an opportunity to advocate for another person:

- 'Have you thought about asking… they're brilliant at these things?'

Saying *yes* when you want to say *no*

Sometimes you may end up saying yes when you want to say no. Perhaps your boss has asked you to complete a task and saying *no* may be a career-limiting move. Maybe there's something you're doing because it's for a person you care about. Or even you know the experience will be good for you. Understand that you've made the choice to say yes even though your heart is not fully in it. Then participate fully (without being grumpy or moaning) and see if you can eke out a little joy in the process.

The route to WorkJoy – Boundaries

Using the active WorkJoy formula, let's explore some ideas of how you could use the three Es of Engagement, Energy, and Experimentation within the context of **Boundaries** to both cultivate WorkJoy and reframe WorkGloom.

Boundaries	Cultivating WorkJoy	Reframing WorkGloom
Engagement	Direct your thinking towards the what (**situation**) and the who (**people**) when you're setting boundaries rather than towards the boundaries themselves – this will make them more realistic and easier to implement.	Remember that there will always be times when the boundaries go out the window – that's real life. Don't give up because it didn't work one time.

Energy	Invest your energy in defining your **non-negotiable**, **bouncy**, and **free-flex** boundaries to allow different levels of adaptability in real life.	Rather than rushing to an answer and regretting your decision, invest a little time in **pausing** and **pondering** before you **pick**.
Experimentation	Share your boundaries with your colleagues, as it's much easier for people to respect boundaries when they are clear on what they are (e.g., 'Every Thursday I will be leaving at 4pm as it's the day I get to pick my kids up from school' or 'I prefer 50-minute meetings to make sure I'm fully engaged and not rushing to my next one').	Experiment with saying *no* in clear and concise ways instead of creating elaborate excuses!

Now that you've tested your **Boundaries**, let's uncover the **Stories** you tell yourself and other people.

CHAPTER 5

STORIES

Introduction

Stories are everywhere. Whether passed down by word of mouth, printed on paper, or shared via social media, they are at the heart of how humans communicate. When a story exists only in your mind, it's easy for it to get bent out of shape and create things like the dreaded imposter syndrome, chipping away at your self-belief. It took me years to unpick and understand my personal story and even longer to feel ready to share it. It's something that is always evolving, and I now know that I hold the power to create the next chapter of my story and so do you. In this chapter, you'll explore the stories you tell yourself, the ones you share, and how to take control of your narrative.

Your story world

You've experienced stories since before you can consciously remember. From the bedtime stories you were told as a child, to doing 'show and tell' at school. As an adult, you're asked to share your stories at key moments like job interviews – there is much joy to be found in sharing and listening to stories. You hold the power within you to create new narratives, to step out of a story that no longer works. You can flip your stories from woes to wonders, from horrors to hope, and from gloomy to joyful. You can add new and different characters, and exciting adventures to embark on. You can go fast or slow. Don't wait for someone else to write the next paragraph in your story. Pick up the pen, it is yours to craft.

You interact with the stories in your head and the stories of others. A web of information and connection that would be impossible to keep track of, let alone control. The stories in your head have an enormous impact on how you view things and how you feel. Let's dig into some of the core stories and explore how you can create a more joyful approach.

The stories you tell yourself about yourself

These stories hold incredible power to influence your thinking and your actions. Depending on the type of stories you tell yourself, they can be the bedrock on which to build real joy or the influencer of gloom. Without any light to shine perspective on them, with no one to listen to them or challenge them, they can cause all kinds of problems, including **imposter syndrome** and **unchecked arrogance.**

Imposter syndrome has become a popular topic over the last decade. It's that feeling you have when you don't feel good enough, worthy enough, or when you feel like you don't know enough and someone is about to expose your lack of expertise. This can be heavily influenced by the environment you are in. If you're feeling undervalued or that you don't belong, your imposter may be on guard. For many years, people have been told they have imposter syndrome and that's the reason for their lack of 'confidence' or 'progression'. This narrative is starting to be challenged, with organizations realizing that culture is a contributing factor. It is a horrible, exhausting feeling that can influence both how you think about yourself and how you behave. Features of it include becoming hyper-self-aware, over-analysing, and perfectionism.

Unchecked arrogance sits firmly at the other end of this see-saw. Arrogance is thinking (and acting like) you are more important, know more, or are better than other people. This end of the spectrum is rarer and people who sit here are often lacking self-awareness. Being on the receiving end of unchecked arrogance is an unpleasant experience and this makes it challenging to give feedback or encourage change in people who display these behaviours.

There is a difference between confidence and arrogance, and there's also a difference between humility and imposter syndrome.

The antidote to jumping on either end of the **imposter** or **arrogance** continuum is the middle ground of **self-belief** – to have trust in yourself. This does not mean you think you're great at everything or have nothing to learn or improve on. It means that you know your strengths and how to use them. That you can take action to improve. Remember that the WorkJoy mindset includes progress over perfection. Building self-belief can be tricky, especially if you have been underestimating or undervaluing yourself and your abilities for some time. Working on it can be transformational to your levels of WorkJoy.

 Reflection questions

- What stories do you tell yourself?
- Where do you find yourself on the imposter to arrogance spectrum?
- How would you rate your current level of self-belief?

Nurturing self-belief

Think of your self-belief as a plant. You'll need sunlight, oxygen, soil, and water to blossom.

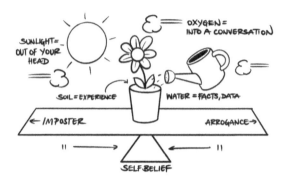

Sunlight: It's easy to get stuck over-thinking, catastrophizing, and putting walls up. Bringing your thoughts out of your head and into the light will help you inject a strong dose of reality and enable you to deal with the story in a progressive way. There are many ways to get things out of your head: some people write them down (journaling, morning pages, and free writing are great tools), some people get artistic (draw, paint, dance, sing), and many people use conversation.

Oxygen: Getting your stories into a conversation with someone you trust breathes life into them. It stops them being out of control fantasies. When done in partnership with someone you trust (see chapter 7), who has your best interests at heart and can talk honestly about their views, it can be transformational. You'll gain much-needed perspective and benefit from the gifts of their thinking, advice, and feedback.

Water: You can add water to your self-belief by seeking out facts, data, and evidence to dispel myths and support growth. It's human nature to focus on what supports your initial thinking (confirmation bias[30]), so seek out

---

[30] J.M. Olejarz, *To avoid confirmation bias in your decisions, consider the alternatives.* Harvard Business Review (5 July 2017). Available from:

data from multiple angles. Get feedback from different people (see chapter 6) as multiple sources create a more balanced viewpoint. Aim for information that enables you to understand what you're doing well and where you can improve. This will help you adapt the story to be rounded and grounded.

Soil: The experiences you choose to give yourself will act as the soil in which you grow. You can choose whether that is rich and fertile, or dry and crusty! Stepping out of your comfort zone and into the learning zone will enable you to learn through your experience, collecting new stories and expanding the pot in which your plant sits.

Your plant may flower best at certain times and in certain situations. At other times, it might be re-seeding itself – getting ready to bloom. The reality is that sometimes you're likely to be pulled in one direction or the other. Whether you need to pull yourself up or rein yourself in, through practice you'll be able to draw upon the stories that have the biggest impact on your WorkJoy.

 WorkJoy story – Imposter to promotion

I'd been working for a large tech corporation for 12 years and was really comfortable there. But in a corporate role, it doesn't matter how high you get, you're only ever doing a tiny part of the overall work. I wanted to do more: ops, compliance, customer care, legal. I wanted more influence. So, from a corporate of thousands, I moved to a business of just 15 people. When you've been the go-to person for others, it's uncomfortable being the one asking the questions. It was a steep learning curve and the biggest thing I had to

https://hbr.org/tip/2017/07/to-avoid-confirmation-bias-in-your-decisions-consider-the-alternatives [accessed 7 September 2022].

> *change to be successful was my mindset. I can be really hard on myself. The WorkJoy tools really helped me see that I had to give myself the same grace I would give my team. I didn't need all the answers.*
>
> *Just over a year later I was offered a promotion to Operations Director. I didn't know another woman in her thirties who was doing that job and imposter syndrome hit me hard. I used the WorkJoy stories exercises to look back over my career, particularly at my first promotion into a management role – a career-defining moment. I was so conditioned to look for the next thing that I'd forgotten I was exactly where I'd spent years wishing I could be. I didn't feel confident that I could do this next role because I hadn't taken the time to look back and see all the progress and change I'd already made. None of it was luck. My bosses weren't asking if I could do this next role; they were asking, 'Will you do it?' Writing my story not only helped me realize that I could, but that I deserved it! All I needed to do was say yes.*

The stories you tell other people about yourself

A strong foundation for WorkJoy is having clarity on what your story is and being able to share it with others. Many people find talking about themselves uncomfortable, so they have an armoury of avoidance tactics in play – from the old switcheroo of 'let's talk about you', to the denial that a story exists at all – there's nothing to see here (as you hide in the corner, looking at your phone, hoping no one notices you are there!).

Crafting your core narrative

Listening with wonder to the stories other people tell and thinking your own is boring or inconsequential is a common theme. Stories are meant to be told and your story is interesting and valuable to other people. Having stories ready in advance of needing them can be useful to:

- Remind yourself of who you are, your journey, your successes, the hurdles you have jumped over, the ways you've grown, and where you're heading to.
- Easily recall and share when someone asks you a question about yourself (a pre-prepared, ready-to-go, engaging version, rather than the put-on-the-spot version).
- Act as the foundation of a conversation about you, your background, your career, where you want to head (helping people to understand how they can help you).

 Reflection questions

What types of stories would you like to have ready to go?

- **Context** – in which situations might you use each type of story? (e.g., an interview or a performance review)
- **Outcome** – what are you hoping the outcome might be? (e.g., a new job or a positive score)
- **Purpose** – what is the purpose of sharing this story? (e.g., to help the panel understand how you'd add value or to share the details of your achievements)
- **Audience** – who will be experiencing your story and what might they want/need from you? (e.g., a hiring panel or your boss)

Core stories

Here are four core personal stories to build, rehearse, and share. They will stand you in good stead and you can apply the theory to any type of story. They will likely contain similar information, variations on the theme of you – with the length, depth, and style changing.

WorkJoy WorkBook

Head to the WorkBook for the Building Your Core
Stories template

Story	Basic structure
My potted history: How I became who I am today	• **Act One:** The Past (Where I've come from and who I was) • **Act Two:** The Present (Where I am now and who I am) • **Act Three:** The Future (Where I'm heading to and who I want to be)
One minute on me: The elevator pitch	• What I do and why I do it • What opportunities I'm after
Future fantasy: Where I'm heading	• What I want the future to look/ sound/feel like • How I plan to get there • What support I need to make it happen
Deep dive: Aka Me 101	• More life-related stuff • My values and beliefs (see more on **Values** in chapter 3) • Where my strengths are and what I've learnt • What I'm working on

Once you have written your story, you need to say it *out loud*.
Your brain connects differently to context when it hears you
saying it than it does when you read it. So, get practising!

The stories you tell yourself about other people

You hold an infinite number of stories in your head about other people that are sourced from your interactions. They can be created in microseconds based on a social media post or in depth from sitting next to a colleague (and everything in-between). These stories may range from being about those you hold dear, to the people you place on pedestals, to those whom you have disdain for. Whether based on myth or a version of the truth, it's likely you have simplified the complexity of human relationships and assigned people as friend or foe, victor or villain.

For those you allocate pedestal status, confirmation bias seeks out and logs the good stuff they do. Ignoring or making excuses for the not-so-good things, your rose-tinted spectacles firmly in place. You might see them as aspirational – trying to emulate them, adapting your story to be more like theirs. At their best, these stories get us motivated to act. At their worst, they create a sense of competition and comparison, a situation in which you may not be able to live up to their standards. The benchmark created in your mind discounts the amount of effort, energy, and time it took them to attain their status. It can make you feel gloomy that your success has not come so easily as you assume theirs did (even if their 'overnight success' took 10 years of sleepless nights to achieve!). The disease of comparititus[31] is one of the most relentless joy thieves that exists in the world.

For the villains, you focus on everything they could possibly do that fits in to the 'wrong' category – criticizing every

---

[31] K. Caprino, *When comparing yourself to others turns self-destructive.* Forbes (18 August 2017). Available from: www.forbes.com/sites/kathycaprino/2017/08/18/when-comparing-yourself-to-others-turns-self-destructive/?sh=62efc4406539 [accessed 7 September 2022].

move they make, with no wiggle room for fallibility. The way they spoke to you at a meeting, or how they completed a task incorrectly (code for differently to how you'd do it), or how they got promoted into the job that 'should' have been yours, to name a few examples. You're not likely to be at your best with people you've assigned to the villain's vault. Then each move they make reinforces your belief that they are simply no good.

If you take step back from these stories, looking at the facts and the evidence versus the bias and balderdash, you will see that all humans are wonderfully flawed. Holding someone on that pedestal of perfection is not helping you (or them). It doesn't allow for real-life ups and downs, for mistakes, for getting it wrong. Likewise, assuming that someone is all bad, because perhaps you simply don't like them, or because they've done or said something you don't like is creating a story that doesn't help build a better relationship.

The way heroes and villains are portrayed in the media, from politics to fiction and films, encourages this binary categorization in real life. Wanting to be inspired by your heroes and blame all your woes on the villains – 'I didn't get promoted because my boss is a terrible person' or 'I did everything my mentor told me, but it didn't work' – is a much easier tale to spin than the complex reality.

That's not to say that other people can't influence your day. There are some personality features that will light you up, help you connect, and raise your joy. There will also be those that simply suck the energy out of you. Being able to know who these people are, why they light you up or bring you down, and how best to utilize your time with them, is very different from making assumptions about them and their traits.

Reflection questions

- Who have you allocated victor status to?
- Who have you allotted to the villain's vault?
- How does this impact your WorkJoy?

If you've got some stories to re-write about others, here are some thoughts on creating a kinder approach.

Engage your empathy

What you experience of others is just the tip of the iceberg. Underneath the water line is a human being with challenges, struggles, and successes. If you see shiny, remember that there's usually a whole load of effort that's created that. If you see darkness, there's usually a reason why. Social media plays a huge role, so if you're following accounts that make you feel like you're not as good as someone else, like you're 'less than' or that you need to change who you are, consider having a good old clear-out of who you're following. Assuming that people are doing the best they can is usually a good way to go.

Track your growth

If comparison is the thief of your joy, then tracking your personal growth can be the giver. Rather than comparing yourself to others, create a pathway for you to compare your own performance against your personal **Goals** (see chapter 11). Ask the question 'Am I better today/this week/ this month/this year than I was yesterday/last week/last month/last year?'[32] Pick a time frame that makes sense for you and be open to the fact that sometimes you might smash it out of the park and other times you will fall behind. The highs and lows are a realistic part of the achievement of any story – personal or professional

Reserve your judgement

Accepting that all humans are a combination of wonderful and flawed, that everyone makes mistakes, gives you room for your own imperfections. The villains in your story are not all bad and your heroes are not as perfect as you may think. Remembering that you exist in other people's stories as much as they exist in yours, you will create a better playground for everyone. One with no wobbly pedestals for people to ascend to and fall off and no dark dungeons to claw your way out of. Space to be human.

---

[32] B. Stallwood with S. Dowd, *Responding to enforced change*. WorkJoy Jam (series 2, episode 2, 13 June 2021) [podcast]. Available from: https://anchor.fm/workjoyjam/episodes/S2-Ep2---Responding-to-Enforced-Change-with-Steven-Dowd-e12ffce [accessed 7 September 2022].

Develop your understanding

Truly understanding the stories of others will help you to debunk myths and create new stories. Perhaps engaging in a conversation with someone you've categorized as a hero may help you to understand the journey that got them there. Maybe making the effort to talk to the villains in your story will shine a light on the reasons why they behave in a certain way.

The stories you tell other people about other people

Stories don't just exist in the vacuum and you're not always the protagonist. Sometimes you're the narrator of stories about other people, telling the audience stories on their behalf. You may have been assigned the narrator role by the lead character in the story or you may have decided to take it on because you have something to say. These stories have the power to do great things and the power to destroy. When you're storytelling, be mindful of the impact of your influence.

Active advocates

If you're advocating, you're talking positively about someone to other people, using your social capital. Perhaps you're in a team meeting and suggest that one of your colleagues would be great at a role needed on a project. Or you know someone has done a great job and want other people to know their strengths. You'll seek out opportunities, share the good stuff – the strengths and skills – and not expect anything in return. You'll do it proactively and purposefully, investing in the conversations about that person because you care about them. Being an advocate is a wonderful way to build WorkJoy.

Idle gossips

On the other side of the coin is the idle gossip. This type of talking about other people is neither purposeful nor positive. It can range from accidental to deliberately destructive, from breaking confidences to breaking spirits. Some people may put this type of 'trash talk' into the banter category. Let's remember it's not banter if you wouldn't say it to their face – and if you would say it to their face, are you 100% sure they would genuinely find it funny or would they just be humouring you? Knowing when to share and when to keep quiet is a skill. If you're ever listening to other people idly gossip, try stepping out of the conversation or stepping in to stop, pause, or add kind words. Gossip is a sure-fire way to end up with some serious WorkGloom (and spread it!).

The stories other people tell themselves about themselves

There's a whole world in other people's heads. You may think they are nailing life or falling apart. Their best might be different from your best. Always be kind.

The stories other people tell other people about you

These are the ones you may be concerned about – how you're thought of and how you're talked about by other people. There is a fine line on this type of story. Being too concerned with what other people say about you can make you try to change in an inauthentic way, moulding yourself in someone else's vision, losing parts of the real you. Care too little and you risk never growing. Taking time to create and share the stories you want people to tell about you can help to mitigate this challenge.

Reflection questions

- What are you famous for in life and work?
- Are these the things you want to be famous for?
- What does this say about how people perceive you?
- If not this story, what story would you like to be told?

The route to WorkJoy – Stories

Using the active WorkJoy formula, let's explore some ideas of how you could use the three Es of Engagement, Energy, and Experimentation within the context of **Stories** to both cultivate WorkJoy and reframe WorkGloom.

Stories	Cultivating WorkJoy	Reframing WorkGloom
Engagement	Remember that there are multiple stories going on at any one time and you are not in control of all of them, yet you can influence many of them (especially the ones in your head!).	Avoid casting people as victors or villains; instead, engage your empathy and respect that everyone has things going on in their life that you don't know about.
Energy	Invest your energy in nurturing your **self-belief** by giving your stories sunlight (get them out of your head), oxygen (talk about them), water (add data and facts), and fertile soil (learning and growth).	Step away from conversations that disrespect other people and invest your energy into actively advocating for your colleagues.

Experimentation	Define your **core narrative** and start sharing it with different people and see how they respond. Then refine and keep building the stories you share.	Keep a **log of praise** you receive and refer to it often. This will realign your focus, remind you of your strengths, and balance out some of the negative stories you may tell yourself.

Now that you've explored your **Stories**, let's focus on **Learning** and investing in your personal and professional development.

CHAPTER 6

LEARNING

Introduction

If you are committed to your ongoing learning and invest in it, it can bring you bucket loads of WorkJoy. I'm a fan of lifelong learning, adopting a 'never finished' approach. The future world of work will value your capacity to learn, adapt, and grow and your **Career** will flourish (see chapter 8). There is much joy to be had both in the process of learning and in the outcomes it produces. In this chapter, you'll explore different ways of investing in your development as well as how to use feedback as a tool for growth.

Constant change and the ability to adapt

The world of work has changed considerably over the last two decades and even more so over the last few years. Being effective is no longer about learning a set of skills or having deep knowledge in one specific subject. When almost every bit of knowledge is available at the click of a button, when you can teach yourself anything via YouTube and when artificial intelligence or machine learning can do most tasks with greater accuracy than any human, what work becomes for us mere mortals will continue to evolve at pace.

The World Economic Forum states that active learning and learning strategies will be amongst the top 10 skills required by 2025.[33] Taking responsibility for your learning will set you up for future success. If you work in a service business, your clients will need you to stay ahead of the curve and to advise them with the future in mind. If you're a leader, the ability to inspire your people will become even more critical. The days of relying on your IQ (intelligence quotient) are long gone. Your EQ – emotional intelligence – is no longer an addition, or a nice to have – it's essential to your success. Your ability to learn – your LQ – will become critical to success, enabling you to adapt to the ever-changing world.

 Reflection questions

- What's changing in your world of work?
- Where are you on the curve (behind, on track, leading edge)?
- How much Engagement, Energy, and Experimentation have you put into your learning so far?

Play the long game

Whether you're just starting out in your career, working through the leadership ranks, or nearing the final stages of your working life, you can invest in learning and reap the rewards. Try imagining investment in your personal, professional, and career development as a savings account or a pension plan. What you put in now will pay off later, with compound interest. You are the only person who can make the choice to invest in yourself. Sure, your **Boss** may

---

[33] K. Whiting, *These are the top 10 job skills of tomorrow – and how long it takes to learn them.* World Economic Forum (21 October 2020). Available from: www.weforum.org/agenda/2020/10/top-10-work-skills-of-tomorrow-how-long-it-takes-to-learn-them/ [accessed 7 September 2022].

be able to support you (see chapter 10). You also may be in an organization that has brilliant development support, or it could be really limited. Don't limit your learning to what is offered to you; go beyond the basics, and seek to expand your expertise and supercharge your skills. One great thing about living in the 21st century is the smorgasbord of learning opportunities out there, many of which are free!

Blockers, begone!

Let's address some of the blockers that might get in the way of you fully committing to investing in your learning.

I'm too busy... how on earth will I fit learning in?

You have work demands coming from every angle and are juggling too many priorities. You have a life beyond work – family you'd like to spend more time with, hobbies / sports / activities you'd like to have space to engage with, how on earth will you fit in learning too?

I don't know what to focus on... there are too many options!

There are so many options and opportunities, you don't know where to best invest your energy. You get lost in the world of online learning opportunities, with big menus and little clarity on the right route, style, or method for you.

I don't know where I'm heading...

You don't really know where you're heading in your career – so how can you know what to focus on. You don't want to waste your investment by heading in the wrong direction, so you stand still and wait for the answer.

Reflection questions

- Which of these blockers resonates with you?
- What are the things that stop you focusing on learning?
- What is the impact of being blocked?

Whatever your blockers, working through them will enable you to level up your learning. Address them with gusto and tackle them head on. They are genuine reasons to get stuck. They are also great excuses that can stop you focusing your time and energy on the right things. Try asking yourself this question:

Reflection question

- What percentage of this is genuine reason and what percentage is excuse?

You might find it's a combination of both reason and excuse. For the genuine reasons, there will usually be a logical solution, a sensible path to unblocking that will move you from stuck to started. It may not be easy, but it will be worth it. Getting unstuck could involve planning in the time to get your learning on the agenda. Or committing to working through the overwhelm of too many options, filtering and working out the right development for you. It might also be saying 'not now because life and work are just too much', then deciding when will be the right time. There is a big difference between ignoring the need and deliberately putting it on ice. Timing is always critical. For the excuses, you'll likely need to look deeper and address your mindset.

Reset your definition of success and your success factors

You're probably someone who's worked hard to get where you are today. You did things the way people said you 'should', you tried hard, and worked your way through and up in your career. Earlier in your career, it was clear what you needed to learn to get where you needed to be. Now you are here, trying to build a life, have a career, and the rules of the game have changed. There is no longer clarity that says if you do ABC (e.g., a qualification), you'll get XYZ (e.g., the dream job). You're expected to lead your own learning, work out what you need and invest precious time and energy into it.

Reframing how learning fits into your life and resetting your success factors can help you create a more realistic path to WorkJoy. Learning at work isn't about winning, it's not a set moment in time and it's not an exam to pass. Think about inputs, efforts, and agility over immediate results and outcomes or answers. Consider how you will recognize when you've made that achievement when it isn't as obvious as a pass or fail, or a certificate to prove you've achieved a standard. Once you can clearly describe what success looks like to you, you'll better be able to align your learning with your bigger goals and create goals for your learning.

 Reflection questions

- What does success look like for learning in the context of your working life now?
- How will you know when you get there?

Diversify your development

Getting stuck in a rut with your development may be limiting your potential. Learning doesn't just happen in formal training or workshops. It's not just about the core learning your profession suggests you do, to stay qualified or licensed, or to fulfil your continued professional development (CPD) responsibilities. It doesn't even have to be for work or career purposes, it could be learning a new hobby. Learning can be so joyful, especially if you take the pressure off of it all being about work and allow yourself the freedom to not be good at something. There is joy to be had in dabbling.

Your development happens every single day, if you notice it and if you take a beat to reflect upon it. Charles Jennings, a leading thinker in the world of learning and development, suggests that the formal learning, the classroom (or Zoom-room) learning, makes up about 10% of your learning time and potential. He suggests that 20% is about learning through others, that is, the conversations you have with your colleagues, mentors, or bosses. The rest, a whopping 70%, is gained through your on-the-job experiences.[34] The work you're doing every day, your real-life challenges and problem solving.

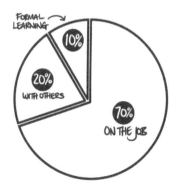

---

[34] J. Arets, C. Jennings, and V. Heijnen, *What is the 70:20:10 model?* The 70:20:10 Institute. Available from: https://702010institute.com/702010-model/ [accessed 7 September 2022].

You don't have to fully subscribe to the exact percentages to engage with this idea, it is simply a useful guide to remember to maximize the opportunities. It could mean one week you're on a course organized by your workplace, the following week you're at an industry networking event. Then another week you're reading an article and the following week you're listening to a podcast.

If you apply an 'every day is a learning day' mentality, it's almost guaranteed that you will find learning in everything you do. From a conversation with friends, to watching your favourite TV show or reading some fiction, there will be inspiration. If you've switched on your learning brain, there will be moments when a character says something and suddenly all the dots connect and the piece you've been missing in a puzzle appears.

There are many ways to develop so don't limit your learning – explore and experiment. The magic trick is to find a combination that works for you and fits into your life. A selection of activities and actions that become a learning habit and help you become a lifelong learner.

 Reflection questions

- Where are you currently focusing your learning attention, effort, and investment?
- What areas have you not explored recently?
- What are the opportunities to diversify?

Maximize the micro

Learning doesn't have to be long and arduous; it can be surprisingly short and simple, to fit into your life.

If you like your numbers, here's some that really add up!

- In the UK there are on average 255 working days per year.
- If you complete just 10 minutes of learning per official working day, you'll have completed 2,550 minutes of learning over the year.
- That's 42.5 hours or a whole average working week's worth for 10 minutes a day of effort.

Try out some of these 10-minute learning ideas and you may find that the learning buzz gives you a little WorkJoy boost.

Ten x 10-minute learning ideas

1. Watch half a TED talk
2. Start reading a chapter of a book
3. Read an article from a publication related to your role
4. Engage in a quick conversation with an expert
5. Start a podcast episode and listen to 10 minutes a day
6. Notice how someone you admire does their work (without looking like a stalker)
7. Take a notebook and pen when you watch TV and write down a quote/action
8. Ask someone to help you with a task
9. Watch a YouTube tutorial
10. Write down your learning points for the day

Schedule the structured

There's the bigger stuff too, the day-long training courses or development programmes, requiring deep focus, for which space must be found. To make the most of these, get them scheduled into your diary. Sign up to the courses you must complete sooner rather than later. Book on them as soon as you've set your **Goals** (see chapter 11) and know that this is a critical piece of the puzzle. Don't wait until you've only got a week to complete your CPD, when you're drowning in your to-do list. Block the time for these things out in your diary ASAP and protect them as you would any special occasion. Then, and this is possibly the hardest bit...

- Commit to it...
- Show up to it...
- Engage with it...
- Be all in!
- Don't move it...
- Don't not show up...
- Don't show up but be doing 12 other things at the same time...
- Don't show up and drop off for an urgent call...

Not fully committing is undervaluing yourself and the importance (and potential WorkJoy) of your personal, professional, and career development. You are worthy of this time, and you are worthy of growth.

 WorkJoy story – Pigeon steps vs giant strides

I've spent much of my career working in sport and have been lucky enough to gather advice from the best coaches in the world. One that has stayed with me is that if you're not actively working on yourself, you're actually falling behind. I try to live this in my working life, and I always seek out the learning. For example, there's always something new to learn on MS Excel, and the internet always has a guide or video. This way I'm learning in little doses, sometimes so small I don't even think of it as development – I'm just getting better at my job.

I know I also need to take the giant strides. A few years ago, I moved into a new role, in a specialism I hadn't worked in before. It's where I had been aiming to get to for some time, so it was a great move for me. Working with people from this new area, I heard that a specific course and qualification had been career making for many people. I researched it and knew this was the right big learning for me. Yet, the timing wasn't quite right for the next intake. It was a 9-month commitment with lots of work to be done in the evenings and weekends. I was getting married in that time frame and knew I wouldn't be able to give it my all. So, instead, I set a goal to do it the following year, when I'd have more space.

When the time was right to apply for the course, I went to my employers with a business case asking them to financially support me to complete the course. It's not something they've ever considered doing before but I figured the worst they could say was no! My business case explained how my learning would improve how I did my job and they ended up (after a bit of negotiation!) paying 50% of the course fees for me. By waiting a year, I was able to fully commit to it and I'm very proud of my achievement. It's a qualification that will stand me in good stead for my next career move. I've got my sights set on the next big learning programme, and again, it's about timing as I'm now a Dad and I need to plan around my little one!

Now that you've considered the mindset for learning, let's explore one key development factor – feedback. Whether the word feedback fills you with dread or gets you excited to learn more about yourself, it can be the key that unlocks growth, development, and change.

Feedback focus

You may not yet get enough feedback or receive it in the right way to really capitalize on it. It's not always wrapped up nicely or labelled as feedback. Often, it's just a conversation you've had with another person who's highlighted something you're great at and/or something to work on. Even the label 'feedback' can create a sense of fear, especially when it's noted as 'negative' or any of the words that have (not so subtly) replaced the negative with such as 'developmental', 'growth', or 'direct'. Your mind may send you to that negative place, where you assume that the news will be bad, creating a disproportionate response. You then focus on the stuff you could be better at, rather than enhance the things where you excel, where you feel aligned, and where you find your joy!

The first thing to work on is that all feedback is simply information to help you understand the impact you have. Whether it's delivered beautifully packaged or handed to you in a dodgy old plastic bag, in a befuddled and bungled way – it's there to help you. Stop judging how it is given – you cannot control the behaviours of other people. You can only control how you respond. Sometimes the beautifully wrapped gift is a load of old rubbish on the inside. Inside the dodgy bag may be the gem that could change your attitude, your approach, and enable your ambitions to be realized. Remember that feedback about you belongs to you – it's up to you to actively seek it out, to be open to it when it comes, and, the most critical thing – to do something about it!

Understanding your feedback feelings

Let's go back in time and remind yourself that you're already good at taking on board feedback and doing something with it. You've been responding to feedback since the day you were born. From the people who raised you, to your education, and throughout your working career. Do you remember how you learnt to walk, talk, or ride a bike? You did it by trying, failing, getting feedback, trying again, adapting, getting more feedback. On and on until you got it. Then, when you had it, you practised and used the skills until they became natural to you.

Your experience of feedback so far will influence how you feel about, respond to, and act on feedback you receive.

Ask yourself these questions and give yourself a score to discover where you may want to pay some attention:

 WorkJoy WorkBook

You can find the Feedback Self Assessment in the WorkJoy WorkBook

Feedback self-assessment

How comfortable are you at accepting compliments and praise?				
1 Very Uncomfortable	2	3	4	5 Very Comfortable

How comfortable are you at reflecting and responding to critique?				
1 Very Uncomfortable	2	3	4	5 Very Comfortable

How often do you actively seek out feedback?				
Weekly	Monthly	Quarterly	Annually	Rarely

How often do you actively give feedback to others?				
Weekly	Monthly	Quarterly	Annually	Rarely

How often do you act on feedback you are given?				
Always	Regularly	Sometimes	Rarely	Never

How often do you loop back and share what you've done because of feedback?				
Always	Regularly	Sometimes	Rarely	Never

Perhaps you're comfortable with seeking out feedback. Maybe you love getting praise or you're great at giving it. You could be struggling with acting on it or finding the tough stuff hard to handle. Wherever you are, read on for some thinking and tools to help you become a feedback pro.

Gathering feedback

When it comes to gathering feedback, let's start with who you get it from.

Feedback friends

You don't need feedback from 100 people, you need a few **feedback friends** (FFs) who are able to observe you in the real-life situations you encounter. Think about the people you either trust or admire (or both). Pick people who will be both honest and direct with you, not those who will fluff it up to avoid hurt feelings. You want people who are on your side and want to help you be even better at being you – not to change you into someone else. You may find certain people in your **Squad** are ideal for this role (see chapter 7). Choose a challenger if you want some 'how could I do this better?' feedback and a cheerleader if you need a quick confidence boost!

You would be wise to avoid:

- **The Fans** – they will be too influenced by their rose-tinted spectacles and their impression that you are just wonderful to be truly honest with you.
- **The Foes** – they will be too influenced by their less than impressive perception of you to consider that you could ever do anything well.

If you don't ask, you don't get…

Don't be afraid to ask people directly and in advance, being as specific as possible to enable them to focus their feedback. Make your request small and related to your development goals. For example, before you…

- … send an important report, ask a FF whom you admire for their concise writing to give it the once over and provide you with their thoughts
- … step on stage for a big presentation, ask a FF who is a great orator to take notes on how you came across on stage
- … attend an important meeting, ask a FF who will be in the meeting to feed back afterwards on how well your questions were structured

Sometimes you might worry that you're asking too much of someone, or you're taking up too much of their valuable time. Remember that it's a massive compliment to them that you respect their opinion on your performance. If they don't have time or can't offer you what you need, the ball is in their court to say no. You'll likely find people say yes more than they say no if you ask.

 Reflection questions

- Who might your feedback friends be?
- What would you like your feedback friends to give you feedback on?
- In what situation can you ask them to help?

The compliment conundrum

Sometimes feedback, especially praise, is too vague to be useful. 'Well done', or 'great work' may give you a serotonin rush of success (and a micro-moment of WorkJoy), yet it has little lasting effect or any ability to truly enhance your performance. The solution to the conundrum is to alchemize the compliment into feedback. When someone offers you a compliment, simply say something like this (obviously make it your own, using your authentic voice and language that feels natural to you!):

'Thanks so much for that, I'm grateful for your feedback. Would you be able to tell me more about what specifically was good so that I can understand at a deeper level?'

This way, rather than just feeling good, you'll learn precisely what you are doing well so that you can do it more or apply it in different situations.

Please (don't) praise me!

Many people find it excruciating when people offer them praise, preferring instead to hear the tougher stuff. This may lead to a tendency to:

- Dismiss the compliment entirely ('oh it's nothing' / 'I was just doing my job')
- Deflect the compliment to someone else ('oh it was a team effort' / 'you should really be thanking…')
- Self-deprecate

This kind of reaction puts people off giving you feedback in the future, limiting your development. The same applies if you react, perhaps by being defensive or finding excuses, to the tougher stuff.

Get WARM

Here's a very simple process to train your brain to respond well to *any* feedback you receive, and all you need to remember is WARM:

W	Welcome the feedback with an open mind	Show you're open to feedback by asking for it and giving people advanced permission to share their thinking with you.
A	Accept it with an attitude of gratitude	Train yourself to say 'Thank you' to the feedback giver. Accepting it doesn't mean you have to agree with it, it means you're grateful to have received it.
R	Reflect on the information provided (see Let the feedback ferment, below)	Take some time to reflect (you don't have to have an immediate reaction or answer) and then consider your response.
M	Make a plan of action	Create a plan of what you will do with the information. Remember to loop back to the feedback giver so they're not left wondering!

Let the feedback ferment

To be able to grow from feedback, the first step is to reflect on it. Here are some reflection questions and some thought starters, that can help you unpick and learn from feedback. Perhaps think of a piece of feedback you've recently received and use this as an example to work with:

 Reflection questions

What does this feedback tell you about my strengths, preferences, and development areas?

- Does it make you feel pleased, proud, or puzzled?
- Is it direct and clear or is it vague? Do you need to ask more questions to really understand it?

- Is it a pattern of praise you should be proud of? Should you be adding this to your praise log so you can start to really believe it?
- Is it a reminder of a development area you could work on? Have you started work on it? Do you know what to do? Who could you ask for help?

What other information do you have to support this feedback as a fact or dispel it as a myth?

- Is this new information or old hat?
- When/where/from whom have you heard this message before?
- What other evidence do you have that supports or dispels this?
- Do you believe it? Are you right in your belief or are you hiding from something?

Who does this feedback come from?

- Does this feedback come from a fan, a friend, or a foe?
- Do you trust and respect the person giving the feedback to you?
- Could this feedback help you develop a constructive relationship?
- How would you feel about sharing your plans and progress with them? (This will tell you about the level of trust you have.)

How does this feedback relate to what you already know (or are discovering) about yourself?

- Does this feedback confirm or conflict with your perspective of who you are?
- Could it be useful to your growth?
- Is it a potential blind spot for you?
- Does it tell you something about what you want to keep or do more of?

Feedback is like a muscle – the more you exercise it, the stronger it becomes, and the better you will be at getting, giving, and growing from it. Like everything in life, the more you do it, the more you'll find your special way of doing it well. It's something you should be practising daily.

Regularly reflect

The act of learning is massively enhanced by reflection, and it doesn't need to be hours of navel gazing or serious contemplation. At the end of your working day, you could ask yourself the question: **What did I learn today?** Then write it down. A couple of sentences at most. If you're an avid journaler, perhaps habit-stack it into that activity (see chapter 11). If you're digitally minded, create a space to log your learning. When you first build your reflective practice, you'll be pleasantly surprised at how much learning you're doing already – perhaps you've just never labelled it as learning before?

The route to WorkJoy – Learning

Using the active WorkJoy formula, let's explore some ideas of how you could use the three Es of Engagement, Energy, and Experimentation within the context of **Learning** to both cultivate WorkJoy and reframe WorkGloom.

Learning	Cultivating WorkJoy	Reframing WorkGloom
Engagement	Spend some time considering what your new learning success factors are and direct your plans towards these desired outcomes.	Avoid thinking that learning is an arduous task and redirect to a micro-learning approach.

Energy	Invest your energy in being an active feedback seeker and giver (e.g., schedule a daily reminder in your calendar saying 'what feedback have I asked for or offered today?').	Plan in when you'll do your 10-minutes of learning each day and build a bank of easily accessible learning materials so that you're not wasting time searching for them (e.g., have your podcasts downloaded or keep a book in your bag, etc.).
Experimentation	Try using the WARM method when you receive feedback and use the reflection questions to really understand what it means for you. Then, always take action! (e.g., with this feedback I'm going to change/implement/do...)	Experiment with diversifying your learning using the 70/20/10 thinking – this will keep your learning fresh and help you avoid getting bored with one style (e.g., always doing e-learning).

Now that you've explored your **Learning,** let's move to part 3, and focus on some critical areas to pay attention to, starting with the people in your **Squad.**

PART 3

THE OUTER WORKJOY FACTORS

CHAPTER 7

SQUADS

Introduction

To create and maintain WorkJoy, you need people around you who can provide you with high levels of support and great challenge to keep you growing – these people are your squaddies. If you invest in these relationships, they will help you create a working life that is truly full of joy. It isn't about who likes you or who your work friends are. Better labels might be professional partners, active allies, or constructive colleagues. I credit my squad with enabling me to be brave and ready to take on any challenge life throws at me! In this chapter you'll look at how to build an effective squad, how to utilize your wider network, and who to avoid (those moodhoovers)! Let's explore how you can build and maintain a truly powerful squad.

Diversity in your squad

Humans are naturally drawn to people who are like them – it's called affinity bias.[35] It's rooted in the need to feel safe and have a sense of belonging.[36] It means you can unwittingly end up with networks that are filled with carbon copies of yourself. This type of homogeneous grouping may give you

---

[35] J. Caccavale, *What is affinity bias and how does it affect the workplace?* Applied (6 May 2021). Available from: www.beapplied.com/post/what-is-affinity-bias [accessed 7 September 2022].

[36] O. Eastwood, *Belonging: The ancient code of togetherness* (2022).

that sense of safety, yet it is unlikely to give you diversity in thinking, in advice, and in skills.

Your squaddies don't have to be people you work *with*, they can be family, friends, colleagues, ex-colleagues, etc. There will be squaddies who know you deeply, with years of shared history, and others who may only know you vaguely, having very limited exposure, giving you both fresh perspectives and deep knowledge. One squaddie may be on a similar career path to you (alongside, ahead, or chasing your tail) and another may be from a totally different industry. By including people from outside of your organization or industry and beyond your role or team, you'll bring in the brilliance of the naive expert. Of course, it's very useful to have people who are there alongside you, as that shared knowing can be a powerful source of support.

You can make your squad a richer source of support by stepping out of your own demographic box. Diversity of family background, gender, race, religion, socio-economic status, disability, neurodiversity, and culture can bring alternative thinking. This can also be gained through working with people from a range of geographical areas as well as those who speak different languages. Simply sharing thinking using a different vocabulary can lead to an expansion of thinking. You may have people who are at a similar life stage to you, or people who are the wise owls with years of hard-earned experience and advice to share. It is also worth seeking out the perspective of people who are newer to the world of work, who haven't been through it all already. A diverse squad can help you understand dynamics at play like power and privilege – opening your eyes to previously unnoticed elements.

Squad positions

Let's look at your role in the squad before moving on to explore six key squad roles.

Headliner

You are the headliner, the protagonist, the lead singer (whichever metaphor works for you!). You have hiring and firing rights. You'll need to engage your squad and be ready to lead them, being clear about what you need. Your squaddies aren't mind-readers, they're busy living their own lives, so you may need to be quite direct about how important they are to you. A squaddie is a significant relationship that deserves more than a cursory moment of attention when you need something from them. Properly nurturing your relationship is an essential duty of a squad leader. A squad that is unclear on its roles or one that is not looked after is just a group of people you know. It's never a bad thing to have a passive network, you just won't get as much out of that group as you will an engaged squad!

It's essential that you don't see this as a one-way street. Keep in mind the questions 'What can I offer to my squaddies? What position could I hold in their squad?' You may not be the right fit for them and their needs. Don't give up if you're not anointed into their squad – it's not rejection, it's selection. Maybe it's not the right time and you will be needed in the future. Instead, why not pay it forward and offer your squad services to someone who needs your unique blend of skills (proactive reciprocal squadding is advanced level WorkJoy!). There is real joy to be found in giving and you'll find the more you give, the more you'll get[37] – the joy of reciprocity! There is a very simple way to

---

[37] A. Grant, *Give and take: Why helping others drives our success* (2014).

become a great squaddie, you just add 'what can I do to support you' to every conversation you have.

Six squad roles

Let's work through six suggested squad roles as a starting point. You may find you'd label them differently or add additional roles to meet your unique needs. Every person will bring their own personality and style, so two people who play the same role may give you very different types of support. You might not need all six roles and you're unlikely to need all of them all the time. There are also rarely spotted squaddies who, by the nature of their role (and their personalities), may pop in and pop out of your life at opportune moments. Some squaddies may know each other, and others may never meet. Unlike a work-based team, the various levels of interaction between the players can be of benefit.

Some of the humans in your squad may be specialist, with skills aligned to a specific role, and others may be more generalist, switching hats as they go. Like any great team, they will bring their individual strengths and be able to complement each other's skills. When a squad is well enabled, it will provide support that is greater than the sum of its parts.

As you explore the roles, you'll immediately recognize the positions some people in your life are playing – it will be obvious. Other squaddies may be quietly supporting you without you even recognizing it (yet). You'll likely have roles without a person and people without clear roles.

 WorkJoy WorkBook

You'll find the Mapping Your Squad template in the WorkBook

Here are the six roles and what role they perform:

 Cheerleaders

- A cheerleader always sees the good in you, focusing their attention on your strengths
- They build you up and openly talk about what you do well
- They are who you go to when you need a pep talk or a self-belief boost
- They don't have to be 'in it' with you, they can stand apart from your work

 Challengers

- A challenger gives you the feedback and advice you need to grow, learn, and change
- They look you in the eye and give you the home truths
- They hold you accountable for making progress

- They are your point of call when you need no-holds-barred guidance

 ## Comrades

- A comrade is in it with you, right by your side, experiencing the same things as you
- They offer unwavering commitment to you through good times and bad
- They are always there for you whatever you need
- They are your first call when you succeed and when you have a crisis

 ## Creatives

- A creative helps you to spark ideas, consider alternative options, and define solutions
- They offer questions to get your brain engaged
- They share their insight from a different viewpoint, expanding your thinking
- They are the people whom you call when you're stuck in a rut or in a set way of thinking

 ## Connectors

- A connector locates the people you need and introduces you to them
- They have a radar for who could help, support, and guide you
- They generously use their vast personal network to enhance your network
- They are the person you go to with the question 'who can help with…?'

 *Conjurers*

- A conjurer creates the magic that makes you feel optimistic, determined, and brave
- They have an indescribable quality that emanates a combination of warmth and strength
- They provide you with the tools to do what you need, even when it's hard
- They appear and disappear in a puff of smoke when they have worked their magic

Now that you understand more about the roles, consider these questions, and map your current squad.

 Reflection questions

- Where do you have strength in your squad?
- Where could you do with more support?
- Who might you want to add to your squad?

 WorkJoy story – Activating my squad

When I moved into a more senior position at work, I felt I really needed to make a mark, so I embarked on a change management project that would make a huge difference to my team at the hospital where I work. Using the WorkJoy way, I wrote an action plan for what I needed to do and realized it was all about identifying and mobilizing my squad.

Reviewing my squad was really interesting. I quickly identified who had my back, but I also found that there were a lot of repeated names, including one who came up three times. Luckily, I was able to work out what role this person would work best in. I also saw I was lacking a conjurer. Someone to really help me bring things to life! There was one person whose name came up three times; in the end I decided she had equal qualities to bring to each squad 'role' so actually used her for several different aspects of my project… she has so much experience and I think using her in this flexible way meant I have learnt more from her than I would have if I had tried to keep her in one role alone.

In order to move my project on and deal with problems as they came up, I literally wrote a list of who in my squad I needed to speak to each week and worked through it systematically. I'm a methodical person so I knew that approach would work for me. The project was a great success. I ended up merging my ideas with a different team who were working on a similar idea and together we managed to implement the changes I had envisaged.

Squad membership

A great squad is not set in stone; it can flex.

Your 'lifer' squaddies

Some squad members become central characters in the story of your working life. Perhaps you'll have three or four core people who play multiple roles and stick with you. One challenge you may come across with your lifers is that they become very close to you, which can lead to issues like making assumptions and being overprotective. Watch out for this in your squad.

Your 'reason and/or season' squaddies

You may bring people into your squad for a specific reason. Perhaps supporting a transition point in your life or an essential skill to help with a particular challenge. Maybe you bring in a mentor to help you connect across your industry. Or you need more challenge than you can get from your lifers (because they love you too much), so you invest in a coach to get that external perspective. Squaddies can be like fixed term contractors; they come for a specific season and head off once things change. Instead of lamenting their loss, be grateful for their presence.

It's worth doing a regular squaddie audit. Perhaps someone who was once a comrade is now better placed as a challenger, for example. It can also lead to bringing new people into your squad when you identify a gap and are craving a different type of support. There will be times when you need to say au revoir to squaddies, due to a change in situation or circumstance – like moving jobs or becoming someone's **Boss** (see chapter 10).

Right sizing your squad

Too big a squad is unwieldy, and you won't be able to pay as much attention to everyone. Too small and you might end up asking too much of some people or needing a different skill set. It's a fine balance of small enough to develop and maintain relationships of trust and care (which take investment) and big enough to fulfil the roles you need. If you're in a status quo phase, you might want a small, core squad. If you're looking to make a career move, are going through a challenging time, or are making any kind of transition, you may want a larger squad. The more you work with your squad, the more experience you'll have of finding the right combinations of people for the right moments in time. It's not an exact science, it's a fine art!

Building your squad

When reviewing your squad, you may have noticed that you have some gaps or need a boost of different energy. It's time to actively search out and recruit some new members for your squad by asking for help. Here's how.

1. Pick a role you would like to bolster in your squad and define the skills you are looking for.
2. Identify some people who might fit the bill – your active network might be a good place to start (see below).
3. Book in time to meet with them and talk.

Many people find asking for help to be awkward, yet it is something we often admire in other people. The worst that can happen is they say no. They might:

- Be having a bad day (we all get them)
- Not have any time to give support (a full schedule and working on their boundaries)
- Think someone else is better placed to help (ask them who and for an introduction)

Remember that rejection may feel awful, but it is usually short-lived. Regret for not doing something often lasts a lot longer and can eat away at your self-belief.

It's unlikely that someone you have a limited relationship with right now will go straight to a core squaddie. Start by asking them for their help in something *small*, something *specific*, and something *simple* for them to do.

Try this three-step process:

1. Share the context and where you see their strengths (share your feedback).
2. State the challenge you need help with (declare your goal).
3. Ask for what you need (remembering to keep it small, specific, and simple).

For example: You want to build your challengers and are keen to be better at speaking up in meetings (a development goal). You've identified someone who you admire for doing this well. When you meet with them, you might say something like this (after you've warmed up with the normal social etiquette and in your own words!):

1. I really admire how you always speak up in our meetings. The way you structure your thoughts and share them in such a concise way is where I want to get to.
2. I often leave meetings wishing I'd said something, and I've made a commitment to say at least one thing in each meeting going forward.
3. Would you be able to share with me how you structure and share your thoughts whilst in the room?

Nurturing your squad

Once you've identified your squad, it's time to make sure you nurture your relationships. Practising gratitude can make you happier[38] and it encourages your squaddies to know that their efforts aren't wasted. Pick one person with whom you want to nurture your relationship. Set up a time to meet or talk – a quick coffee on Zoom would be sufficient. Then share directly with them how they have helped you and the impact they have had. Try this three-step method to structure your feedback:

1. Thank them for what they give you – being specific.
2. Share how it made you feel (yes – feelings!).
3. Describe the impact their support has on you.

---

[38] E. Stoerkel, *The science and research on gratitude and happiness*. PositivePsychology.com (4 February 2019). Available from: https://positivepsychology.com/gratitude-happiness-research [accessed 23 June 2022].

	Example 1	Example 2	Example 3
Thank you for...	advocating for me to take on that project	being there for me when I needed a shoulder to cry on	telling me what I needed to hear
You made me feel...	confident to take on a new challenge	able to have a real, human moment when I was upset	reflective and empowered to make the changes
... and the impact was...	my boss has now seen my leadership skills in a new light	that I was able to be kind to myself	I have now upped my game

Your network

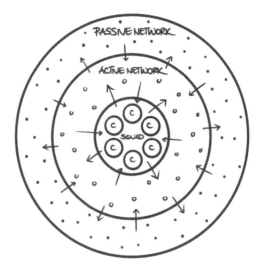

You also have a network which can be much broader in size and scope. Much like the difference between friends and acquaintances, your squad and your network will play different roles. Your **squad** is the central part of your network, built on strong relationships with high-touch connections. Your network emanates outwards from there.

The second ring is your **active network**. You know them and they know you. They may not be regular features, yet an email or call from you or them would get you together. Often this group is filled with people you've 'done stuff with' (working, studying, etc.). Some may also be friends. This group is the most likely place for you to gather new squaddies from and the place you want to keep them when they move on.

The outer ring is your **passive network**. These are likely to be people you've connected with at some point, yet don't have a relationship with yet. You may have met at a conference or be connected through other people (second-line connections). They may be contacts on social media (your LinkedIn is likely full of passive connections!). Don't underestimate this network, though, especially the second-line connections, as there's power in loose connections.

Networks or networking?

The term networking creates a visceral response in some people. The image of people in shiny suits, eating soggy croissants and being talked at by people trying to sell you something comes to mind. It doesn't paint a picture of much WorkJoy does it? Of course, some people love networking and there's lots to gain from it. If you're at the right type of networking event, with the right people, there is lots of joy to be found. Meeting interesting people, creating new connections, and practising core skills like telling your personal **Story** (see chapter 5), listening, and asking meaningful questions are all benefits of engaging in networking type activities.

If you're a network-phobe, you can build a great network without ever having to go to a networking event. You can do it one-on-one if that's more your style than mingling in a crowd. Attending random events for the sake of networking will be less fruitful than carefully curating a selection of activities. Perhaps your organization or profession has opportunities to meet people through specific ERG (employee resource group) or other events. Maybe it's about getting involved with a subject you care about. Experiment with where you get to meet and interact with people who bring you interesting perspectives.

Now that you've explored who you do want to invest your time with, let's address those that you might want to avoid.

Moodhoovers (aka who to avoid)

Whereas your squad and network are often sources of WorkJoy, there are always going to be people that you find challenging. Some of them may be overtly 'not your people', the people you avoid in the corridor. Others may hide their moodhoover nature in small comments, making it harder for you to identify them.

There are some people you may bucket into the moodhoover category because you don't immediately gel with them. Yet, if you take the time to get to know them, to welcome their different perspectives, they could end up a vital part of your squad. It's also important that you develop an understanding of your own impact on other people – this is a critical tool for a successful working life. It is likely that at some point and for some people you may be a moodhoover. Even if you're the 'life and soul of the party' type, or a positive person *all* the time, to some people that is unbelievably draining. Moodhoovers aren't just moody people!

Understand that not everyone has to be your cup of tea and you will not be to everyone's taste. It's good to know that and accept it. You don't need everyone to be a fan. In the working context, there may be moodhoovers you have to deal with on a regular basis. The key is to know what types of traits to watch out for and how to handle these behaviours.

Let's focus on four types of moodhoover often found in workplaces:

- The moaners
- The one-upmans
- The manipulators
- The my-way-or-the-highway-ers

The moaners

Everyone needs a good moan occasionally – a space to vent. It can be a helpful process in letting things go. This is very different to a chronic moaner, where nothing is ever good enough and everyone and everything is just wrong. Something good happens and they will find a way to make it a bad thing. Then the worst trait of all, they take no personal responsibility for fixing what's creating the moan-worthy situation. Moans come round like a record on repeat, and nothing ever changes. You get stuck listening, trying to help, advising, guiding. You get exhausted. It becomes a source of your WorkGloom.

If you're dealing with a moaner, create a 'no moan zone' around you. After you've listened, ask 'what action can you take to make this better?'. If they act, brilliant – you've helped move someone. If they don't take any action and repeat their moan, try saying something like 'last time we chatted you were going to [insert their defined action here], I'd be happy to talk more once you've seen how that works out for you'. Give it a try. They will likely be shocked. What you are doing is very kindly helping, then setting a boundary that states clearly that you are expecting them to take responsibility.

The one-upmans

These people have always either 'done it better' or 'had it worse' than you. Tell them you've had some success at work, and they'll have already done that, two years ago, with better results. Confide in them about a problem you have and theirs will be far bigger, with extreme consequences. They don't listen, they interrupt, and they make it all about them, making you feel inadequate. They are usually deeply insecure and have built this strategy over many years to protect themselves.

You are good enough; your successes are worthy of celebration and your challenges should be listened to. It's possible they don't know they're doing this, and you need to give them some feedback. If this doesn't work, step away (as far as is possible) and choose to surround yourself with people who build you up, not take you down.

The manipulators

These are the sneaky ones – the wolves hiding away in sheep's clothing. They can lure you in like a fairy-tale baddy, tempting you with their fake friendship. It's likely that they'll make you feel special before getting you to do their dirty work. Perhaps engaging in clique behaviours, the in-crowd, and the out-crowd. You will hear them slagging people off and, at some point, you'll probably hear that they've done the same to you.

This type of behaviour is toxic and it's massively catching. If you engage with it, you will become part of the problem. Even just listening to people degrade others without saying anything is being complicit. Don't do it. If you hear it, try saying 'I don't think talking about people behind their backs is helpful' and walk away. This is a very different type of talking behind people's backs than you get from an active advocate (see chapter 5) – that is joyful, this is mean.

The my-way-or-the-highway-ers

Some people have very strong opinions on what should be done and how you should do it. Depending on things like position, hierarchy, and decision-making practices in your working world, you could influence this, or you may just have to get on with it. Where you do have some influence, you may try and convince people why your way is superior, creating a tug of war. It's not a great way of getting things done or building a relationship.

Sometimes a different opinion gets mislabelled in your mind as a person being difficult. Yet different doesn't have to equal difficult. Instead of jumping in with your way, try exploring their reasoning, see the story from the other perspective (there are always at least two sides to every story). If you can both share your thinking, you may be able to create option three – a better, combined way that utilizes the best thinking from everyone in the room.

 Reflection questions

- What moodhoovers are you experiencing now?
- How is it impacting your WorkJoy?
- What moodhoover behaviours might you see within yourself?

The route to WorkJoy – Squads

Using the active WorkJoy formula, let's explore some ideas of how you could use the three Es of Engagement, Energy, and Experimentation within the context of **Squads** to both cultivate WorkJoy and reframe WorkGloom.

Squads	Cultivating WorkJoy	Reframing WorkGloom
Engagement	Consider what roles you are playing in other people's squads and proactively offer to help (e.g., ask 'what can I do to help you with X, Y, Z?').	Check in with yourself and whether you're demonstrating any moodhoover behaviours (e.g., have you become a moaner? – then do something to change).
Energy	Using the WorkJoy WorkBook templates, spend time understanding who is in your squad now and where you have some gaps to fill (e.g., I'm great for cheerleaders, but need some more challengers).	Invest your energy with the right people, in the right places and on the right subjects rather than attempting directionless networking (e.g., find opportunities to engage with others on subjects you care about).
Experimentation	Try out asking someone to help you with a challenge you're having or a goal you want to achieve. Remember to work with something **small**, **specific**, and **simple**.	Remember to share your gratitude to those who help you, sharing your feedback and letting them know the impact they have had (and feel the joy of reciprocity).

Now that you've explored your **Squads,** let's work on how you can consider how you approach your **Careers.**

CHAPTER 8

CAREERS

Introduction

Wouldn't it be fantastic if there was a set of requirements to work your way through and once you'd ticked everything on the list, you'd walk straight into your perfect job. Unfortunately, most careers just don't work like that and there really isn't a magic career formula as there are so many different factors in play. I've found that there is one feature of people with joyful careers: they talk about what they want. In this chapter we'll look at how careers have changed, the different types of career shapes and how to make your moves more joyful.

Career mindset

The word career evokes expectations of well thought out, planned pathways. Yet careers are messy, confusing, and often slightly random. Changing organizational needs, structures, clients, products, and services, the speed of new technology and a changing workforce in terms of demographics and desires means that what careers looked like even 20 years ago is alien to the experiences of the modern workplace.

The 'job for life' is at the top of the endangered species list. Traditional career ladders providing defined progression only exist in a limited number of professions now. New pathways to progression are complex and can be undecipherable in terms of how you get there. Work is no longer predictable, or about learning a skill and repeating it (see chapter 6), and careers aren't either.

There is a whole world of opportunity, ready and waiting for you to dive into. No longer must you find one thing you're interested in and stick with it for life. If you crave variety, you can have multiple roles with different organizations – either over time or at the same time. If you have a passion you want to pursue, you can create a side-hustle. You can build your own path to a destination of your choice.

Different types of career moves

As careers are rarely linear, it may be worth considering what different types of career moves are possible. This approach looks at the shape of your career and these seven examples are possible in many organizations. When you read them, you'll likely recognize some moves that you have made so far and perhaps be inspired to consider alternative options. They can stand alone, and some can be combined. It's not intended to be an exhaustive list and there will be nuances associated with your own career, different organizations, and industries. Take it as broad thinking and see if it could help you to explore options. Over a working lifetime, some people may only make one type of career move. Others may try all the options out.

 WorkJoy WorkBook

Head to the WorkBook for the Mapping Your Career Moves template

Selectively sideways

These moves are some of the most valuable moves you can make. Often taken up within the same subject matter, area of expertise, or profession, these sideways(ish) moves enable you to build your knowledge, skills, and breadth of experience. They allow for gradual development over time and can expand your horizons by exposing you to different people, skills, and challenges. There are often plenty of opportunities to move in a zig-zag pattern.

These moves can happen within your immediate team, or sometimes beyond into another part of your organization. As you experience new things, your capabilities and self-belief grow, as does your ability to see things from different angles. This comes with a side order of wisdom, a wider network (see chapter 7), and institutional knowledge, which can be career gold dust. Perhaps you'll want to move upwards at some point, and you will be just the rounded candidate needed. Or you'll be able to spot an opportunity to create camaraderie between different parts of the business, creating a new process that makes things more efficient. Maybe you'll build comradery between teams and create a more collaborative culture. All these things are what great reputations are made from and that is a foundation of career success.

The breadth of experience garnered sets you up for career adventures outside of your current organization. That might be a move to another firm, expanding your horizons with different people, products, or services. Or maybe it allows you to develop into a new specialism or industry, having developed new knowledge and skills. You may even discover a gap in the market and set up your own thing to fill that gap.

Tactical trip

In a tactical trip, you apply your skills in a new context, broadening your experience and deepening your under-standing of how you 'do your thing' when the environment has changed. Internally, this could mean moving between a specialist function and a customer function or moving from managing a small project team to a big operation. If you're considering moving organizations, perhaps you'll move from a corporate to the third sector, or from a corporate to a cool new start up. The options for tactical trips are plentiful.

In the new environment, you'll build a wider network and be able to explore a whole new world of opportunities. These are some of the most common of career moves and are often taken up by people with a transferable set of skills. If your skills are in demand, you may also be able to secure a role with increased salary/benefits. In fact, it is sometimes easier to gain a pay rise through a tactical trip than it is to do so by growing within your existing role. Plenty of organizations value breadth of experience in different organizations and industries, yet some have not yet seen the value in this, so don't be surprised if some (rightly or wrongly) ask for you to have industry-specific experience.

Long haul ladder

A ladder career move is associated with a traditional career structure. It involves applying for and/or being promoted into a new role at a more senior level. They can happen within your current workplace or be a part of a move to a new organization. These types of moves most often exist in organizations with more traditional, hierarchical structures. The rungs of the ladder are often easier to navigate and climb in your early career. It's often at the mid-levels where the ladder becomes more challenging and the requirements of what is needed to 'make it' become opaquer.

A ladder move often relies on there being a vacancy to fill. If you're looking in a place with lots of different roles and high levels of people movement, these opportunities can regularly present themselves. If you're in a niche area, a smaller organization, or one with higher retention, it can feel like you're stuck in a waiting room. Perhaps you're ready to take on your boss's job, but they're making no sign of moving? Maybe there's an opportunity at the next level, yet there are 17 of you in the team all vying for the same role. Or one of the most annoying examples: the next role you want has a requirement of management experience. You don't have it (yet) and you can't get it until you get a job which requires it, and you're stuck because there's missing rungs thwarting your ascent.

There are also the ladder moves you craft for yourself – they are a lesser-spotted opportunity, yet they can be a brilliant thing. Perhaps you've noticed a role that's really needed in your team. Maybe there's an opportunity to expand the level and scope of what you do now. Or there's a project role or secondment that could act as a temporary rung on your ladder, getting you that experience you require to turn it from a stop gap to a solid step.

A single-organization, fully ladder-based career is becoming less common as the world of work continues to evolve, organizations get flatter and less hierarchical in structure, and more movement between different organizations becomes the norm.

Executive escalator

In a limited number of industries, the pathway from junior team member to executive leader is still clear, very structured, and in-built as part of the organizational structure. In law, accountancy, some medical careers, and academia, time- and skills-based progression are still the norm. In these cases, the routes are planned for you. You're likely to have to put in the hours in both learning and delivering results at each level. You may have to pitch yourself, present your story, and prove that you are worthy of the next promotion, with each stage becoming more challenging.

A word of caution – Executive escalators and long-haul ladders

Hierarchical structures are built as pyramids. There are more roles and more opportunities at the entry- to mid-level than at the mid-senior level, and the pinnacle of the pyramid is reserved for a very small set of leaders. As you ascend, there is usually a combination of increasing responsibilities and demands placed on you. Additional hours become the norm and expectations change. They sometimes come laden with the lure of more money and benefits, of status within the organization and fancy-sounding job titles, but also with the requirement to manage and lead people. It is rare (yet not impossible) to find a series of ladder moves that allows you to become more and more senior within your specialism, without having increased management and leadership responsibility. Yet managing people is not a guaranteed joy maker. As anyone who's managed people will tell you, it's not all fun and games!

These career moves hook you in and keep you firmly on a predefined path. If you're in one of these careers, take a moment occasionally to check in with yourself and challenge whether the outcome is still what you really want.

Deep dive

There are some roles and industries where depth is the most important feature. Being a specialist on a specific subject matter and being the expert is highly valued. Whether it's your skills or technical prowess, you will know it upside down and back to front. It's likely that your work will be at the core of the business or a key enabler to business success. People will rely heavily on you to apply your expertise effectively and efficiently. Many people who enjoy the experience of deep dives find themselves gainfully employed in this way throughout their careers.

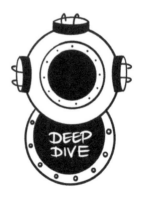

A challenge can be around the traditional progression view of career, and you may not feel that sense of career growth. Some forward-thinking organizations are now finding ways to enable people to develop in these careers (many of them in the tech industry). They're investing in the depth of skill in their organization and rewarding growth within roles, rather than asking them to step out of these roles into management or generalist roles. Let's hope that this type of career path becomes more recognized and rewarded across more industries over the coming years.

Make sure you keep your eyes on the horizon, as being in a specialism or an industry that is changing (and which industries aren't being disrupted?) can leave you desperately catching up. Imagine being a specialist in a specific programming language. You've spent years becoming the best you can be at it, your skills are highly valued, you can take your pick of career opportunities. Then a new language comes along (as they always do) and you were so busy being brilliant at what you do now, you didn't see it coming and wham, you're not ready for the future. So, keep an eye out, keep **Learning** (see chapter 6) and re-specialize yourself before the market forces you to!

Active adventure

ACTIVE ADVENTURE

If you want to mix up what you do, the active adventure may be the right move for you, as you step out of your current role, specialism, or profession. You step in and discover new things, work with different people, in new environments – a fresh challenge. You'll need to learn new skills, develop your strengths, and be ready to throw yourself in at the deep end. There'll be a new language to learn (there's always new lingo and acronyms and shortcuts that leave you wondering if you've landed on an alien planet) and a new culture to investigate.

These moves offer you the opportunity to explore how your skills can be expanded and applied in different settings. They often appeal to people who favour trying new things over deep expertise. Some may say they are riskier moves, as you'll need to push out of your comfort zone. There is also the risk that you could become a Jack/Jackie of all trades, but that's more about how your sell your expedition to future employers. In many places, breadth and diversity of experience is becoming highly valued.

Structured adventures may come in the form of graduate or management development programmes. Often these happen early on in your career, working through different specialisms, developing a breadth of understanding across a business before finding your niche. They can also be in the form of secondments, cover roles, or fixed term opportunities. At the self-led end, they can step you out of employment into the work of self-employment and/or entrepreneurship. There are almost unlimited opportunities if you're prepared to pack your rucksack and head out on an adventure – the world really is your oyster.

Grounded growth

Contrary to popular belief, having a great career is not all about moving role or organization with intense frequency. Great careers can still be made from staying rooted in one type of role and/or in one organization, adding strings to your bow as you grow.

Some people spend their whole careers in grounded growth. Those who value deep relationships that are formed when you stay rooted for a period thrive here. The approach requires commitment to staying up to date, developing skills and expertise – so it's not a stop and stick. It's planting yourself and feeding your roots, allowing yourself to expand into the organizational space.

To make this (un)move work well, you'll need to feel really connected to your role and your organization. Your value to the business will expand as your institutional understanding increases over time and people will be lost without you (although it's important to remember that, often, no role is indispensable – see imbalanced loyalty in chapter 9). There is huge value to having grounded people in organizations and much joy to be had within these roles. You don't always have to be chasing the next big thing.

WorkJoy story – From long haul ladder to active adventure

I'd worked in football for almost 15 years when I was informed that my job was going to be made redundant. It was a really intense and stressful time (I was also moving house!) but I was lucky to have a four-month period in which to work things out. I loved my work, but I'd been shoe-horned into management and really disliked it, so I decided not to apply for any of the positions within my organization. Instead, I wanted to make a change and go after something I wanted to do.

The WorkJoy toolkit helped me work out what I was passionate about. I spotted a history of writing throughout my life; never for a sustained period, but I kept coming back to it in various guises. That was it: I wanted a career in writing, but it never dawned on me that I was capable of setting up on my own. I saw other people starting businesses, and I thought, 'Nope, that's not me'. I thought I was destined to work for other people. But the more I thought about it, the more I realized I had nothing to lose. I had no dependants – it was only me and my cat – so I thought, 'If I don't do it now, I'm never going to do it'.

Through WorkJoy, I found the courage to set up on my own. Within a few months I had a writing business and my first two clients, who I still have today (plus, many more of course!).

 Reflection questions

- Which type/s of career moves have you taken so far?
- What did they give you?
- What might you be considering for your next move?

How to make your career moves more joyful

If you're looking to make any kind of career move, here are some ways to make it happen whilst making it more likely that you'll find and maintain the WorkJoy!

Build your career on solid foundations

There are some things that can have a lasting impact whatever shape your career takes:

- Deliver great work in the job you're currently in
- Do more than the bare minimum
- Display that you can do bigger or different things
- Demonstrate your commitment by doing 'beyond-the-day-job' stuff
- Dedicate yourself to your personal development
- Dare to work like you're already in the job you want

Rest your ladder against the right wall

Consider whether the organization and boss you're resting your career on can provide you with the developmental support you need for your next move. This doesn't mean it's their responsibility to provide you with everything, as your development is always your personal responsibility. Make sure they can enable you and advocate for your career goals. If they can't, you may need to consider resting your ladder on a different wall!

Build your pathway

Being able to define what is needed for a career move and then having it provided to you in a nice, neat bundle is likely to be a pipe dream. Going through the challenge of things like lack of clarity and having to make big leaps is just part of the process. Rather than being annoyed that the provision of career development advice, options, or opportunities isn't offered to you, take that energy, and DIY it. For example:

- Need that management experience? Why not offer to mentor a new starter or get some outside-of-work experience through volunteering (see chapter 2)?
- Want to change careers? Seek out an organization you want to work for and see if you can speak with the team or even job shadow (using your active network to get connected – chapter 7).
- Need to complete a qualification or training course as a prerequisite? Ask your organization to support you with investment or study leave. Seek out grants or other funding opportunities.

Whatever you're lacking, find a way to fill the gap – your future self will be grateful you didn't wait around for someone to do it for you.

Internal vs external moves

Some internal moves are notoriously challenging to make, so it may feel easier stepping into a different organization. Internally, people often have set expectations of you. If you started as a junior member of the team and are now a leader, their stories about you may be out of date. Others may still come to you to do the work you did before. This is normal but niggly. In a new workplace, you can start a new story, with fewer preconceptions.

Moving organizations comes with challenges. It can take months or even years to learn a new role. Building a new network takes time. Navigating different processes, policies, systems, and politics as well as a new culture can be as draining as it is exciting. You will need to weigh up what the right decision is and that's part exploration, part intuition, and part taking a gamble. You will never know for sure, and remember, no career decision is ever final – you can always choose to change it.

Do your due diligence

When another organization wants you, they will put on a show for you. From the shiny recruitment website showing wonderfully happy, well-rested people, to the interviews and offers of free breakfast and flexible culture. The smoke and mirrors may have you signing on the dotted line before you can say 'due diligence!'. Don't be fooled by the flash, look under the hood of the new organization before you sign on the dotted line!

Titles, levels, and remuneration

If you get hung up on job titles, you forget that the joy is in the doing of the job, not in what it's called. A title 'bump' will make you feel good for a day or (if you're in a very title-focused organization) perhaps a week. Getting excited about what you get to do every day because you're learning, growing, and being increasingly more valued has so much more potential joy to be squeezed out of it. That's months, if not years, of WorkJoy waiting for you to grab. In a world where more and more job titles sound like they were made up by an alien playing with a thesaurus, getting hung up on what the name is rather than what you do may be a misuse of your energy.

In some organizations things like grades and levels seem like they're important – a badge of honour. They're used to define what you do and how you can do it and who you can play with at work. That's just the way it is. In others, they wouldn't know what a hierarchy was if it slapped them in the face. It may be very important to other people and not to you. It may be important to you and not others, and it may be important to you *and* others. Whether it is or isn't, don't limit your potential because you don't get the badge.

Your rank does not define your worth or worthiness. The value of your role in society also doesn't equate to your salary (if it did, nurses and teachers and sanitation workers would surely be paid the most?). We exist in a capitalist society and the market sets the monetary value for your role. That value will be different in different industries – almost unlimited in some and very defined in others. If you're waiting for what you offer to be valued more only in terms of rank or remuneration, you're surely on a path to more gloom. Be the person who acts like a leader and doesn't need a number, letter, or badge on their shoulder to be brilliant.

Of course, everyone wants more money. It would be wonderful if there were a magic wand to give everyone the pay rises. There are budgets and limitations. Sometimes a career move comes with additional salary or benefits. Sometimes it doesn't. Sometimes, the best career move you make, the one that sets you up and defines the amazing next steps, the one that brings you regular, consistent joy in your work, is the move where you take a pay cut. One thing to always understand is the market rate for your set of skills, in the industry you work in.

Do the maths

Before you embark on your next career move, make sure the maths adds up in your life. Will the job itself give you the joy you crave in a role – will there be enough of what brings you joy?

Reflection questions

- Are any additional money, status, or benefits going to be enough to offset the extra hours and responsibilities placed on you?
- Will the job allow enough space for your balloon of life (see chapter 2 – **Life**) to invest in other areas?

The route to WorkJoy – Careers

Using the active WorkJoy formula, let's explore some ideas of how you could use the three Es of Engagement, Energy, and Experimentation within the context of **Careers** to both cultivate WorkJoy and reframe WorkGloom.

Careers	Cultivating WorkJoy	Reframing WorkGloom
Engagement	Define what types of moves you've made in the past to anchor yourself in your career story so far and see how it might inform your future.	Consider how any potential career move will fit into your life – and do the maths before you make a move. The grass isn't always greener on the other side.
Energy	Point your energy towards the shape of your possible career moves, rather than specific roles. This can broaden your thinking and open unexplored opportunities (e.g., exploring grounded growth in addition to the deep dive).	If your current remuneration is getting you gloomy, try exploring what your role offers you beyond financial reward (e.g., does it give you flexibility? Are you learning? Do you have a great boss?).

Experimentation	Experiment with DIYing your own career pathway. Seek out potential roles and talk to people about what you're looking for – they may know of just the thing (utilize your **Squad** and your network – see chapter 7).	Invest in doing your current job well, engage (or re-engage) with it, and experiment with reconnecting to the joy you once had. Even if you know you're going to move on, this will help you transition positively into your next role.

Now that you've explored **Careers,** let's look at how the **Organizations** you work with can be a source of WorkJoy... and of WorkGloom.

CHAPTER 9

ORGANIZATIONS

Introduction

Organizations are figments of your imagination. Bear with me on that statement for a moment. I hear people say, 'my company is rubbish at…' or 'if the business could just sort out…', blaming much of their WorkGloom on organizations. Yet, they are not sentient, they are constructs designed to organize (the clue is in the name) how the work gets done. It's the people within them that make decisions and 99% of those are trying their best, often with limited resources and working through challenging situations. They don't get it 100% right (because they're human) and they're not going to be able to meet the unique needs of every employee. Some may be able to meet most of your needs, to give you a great baseline to build WorkJoy on, others may not be your bag and may create a sense of WorkGloom for you. In this chapter, we're going to consider the relationships you have with the organizations you work with and how you may be able to address some of the most common sources of WorkGloom they provoke.

A complex relationship

Your working life has many dimensions and your relationships with different areas can be complex and complicated. You have the work itself, the people you directly work with, your **Bosses** (see chapter 10), customers, clients, partners, and the organization (a firm, a business, a partnership, an enterprise, a trust, an institution, a company, an association). In the pre-digital age, when work was based at a specific place (an office, a hospital, a school, a lab, a site...), we might have referred to the generic term 'workplace'. Yet now, for a lot of people (the office workers in particular) this has become less relevant. Regardless of the name, the organization you work with will inevitably have a large impact on your levels of WorkJoy. The Chartered Institute for Personnel and Development (CIPD) suggests that 'good work'[39] has these six features:

1. Is fairly rewarded and gives people the means to securely make a living
2. Allows for work/life balance (see **Life** – chapter 2)
3. Gives opportunities to develop and ideally a sense of fulfilment (see **Learning** – chapter 6)
4. Provides a supportive environment with constructive relationships (see **Squads** – chapter 7)
5. Gives employees the voice and choice they need to shape their working life
6. Is physically and mentally healthy for people

 Reflection question

- How would you rate your organization against these six areas?

Organizations offer their employees many things, with the most obvious being reward. A regular salary is something people are grateful for, even if it's not the exact number you'd like. For many years, the idea of job security came along with a permanent job, although nowadays the word permanent is probably not an accurate description. Along with benefits like contributions to pension schemes, healthcare, and other

---

39 *CIPD Good Work Index*. CIPD. Available from: www.cipd.co.uk/knowledge/work/trends/goodwork#40068 [accessed 7 September 2022].

financial perks, getting financially rewarded is usually the main reason people have a job. If you're a freelancer or an entrepreneur, perhaps the organization is a client for you, or a business partner, enabling you to run your business. The joys that sit beyond the concept of **work = financial reward** can be considerably broader and deeper.

What brings each person joy from the organizational perspective will be unique to them, yet there are consistent themes; which of these regularly stated reasons resonate with you?

 WorkJoy WorkBook

You can access the Understanding the Joy of Your Organization activity in the WorkJoy WorkBook

 Reflection questions

Which of these sources of WorkJoy would be on your list?

- Making an impact
- Sense of community
- Sense of belonging
- Working with great people
- Working on challenges
- Creating solutions
- Working with interesting clients
- Learning something new
- Having fun

What else would you add?

Whether you're one of 100,000 employees in a global power-house, or it's just you working as a freelancer, where there's work, there's a business-related structure.

The shape of organizations is as varied as the people who work in them. There are firms that are all about profit, some that are all about purpose, others that are about the people, and some are a hybrid of all of these. Some organizations are led by CEOs and boards, many are based on hierarchies, whilst others are matrixed or networked. There are many common features that build joy or have us grappling with gloom irrespective of the organizational purpose, style, or industry.

Let's take a whistle-stop tour of the most maligned organizational features that create WorkGloom. Consider which of these are creating some gloom in your world and consider tackling these with reframing and repositioning.

Life takeover

A phenomenon that often causes WorkGloom is the idea that your whole life belongs to the organization you work with. Because they pay your salary, you become owned by them. Much of this is a **Story** in your head (see chapter 5). Logically, you know that work is a part of life, but it takes up so much time and energy (it's often the biggest balloon – see chapter 2), you may not experience it that way. From getting up earlier to fit in emails before you get stuck in meetings that only add to your to-do list, to trying to make a global call work between time zones and staying up with the owls. Even when you're not working, your brain gets filled with the never-ending list of priorities that squeeze your other priorities to the edges. If you're struggling with life takeover, head back to chapters 2, 3, and 4 to work through what's important in your **Life**, your **Values**, and your **Boundaries** first. This is the central issue that you'll need to work on to create more WorkJoy. And don't forget to engage your **Squad** (chapter 7): this is not one to tackle alone.

Change

It is almost universal that everyone wants something in their organization to change. Yet, when things do change, your brain finds it very hard to handle. There's a difference in how the changes you choose to initiate and those which are thrust upon you feel. Enforced change takes away choices and can leave you feeling disempowered. Organizational change is often too small or the wrong solution to make a difference, so you get disappointed. Or it's too big and it starts to have a major impact, leading us from feeling a little bit peeved that the puzzle hasn't been fixed to a feeling of loss of control. Even the word 'change' can send shivers down the spines of the most resilient of us.

It's a constant feature – from changing customer needs to new technology, structures, and, of course, the pivot (the buzz word for change occurring during Covid-19). It often means breaking something apart and putting it back together in a different way. Rethinking roles and rearranging teams. It can mean losing roles (and therefore people) from the structure. Whether it's your role that gets lost, or the roles of the people around you, it can have a lasting impact. It is unlikely you'll make it through your entire career without being subjected to some sort of organizational change process, so being ready for it, and approaching it with a WorkJoy mindset, may help. One way to help yourself is to accept that you are likely to not be in control of how it plays out. Influence yes, control no. Remember that you are worth more than your job, then put your best foot forwards in whichever direction works for you.

Let's work through some key change challenges that you may need to deal with in your career.

Change challenge: Restructures

Anyone who's been subjected to any kind of restructure, transformation, downsizing, or right sizing will know that it's immensely unsettling. Whether you've seen it coming (and put your armour on) or it's hit you like a tonne of bricks with no warning, the experience can be less than joyful. Even if you agree wholeheartedly (or even half-heartedly) with the purpose of the change, the compelling reasons creating the disruption, it can still hurt. Even the hardiest of people are likely to find a dent in their self-belief if they must work through processes like:

- Re-applying for the role they've been doing for years
- Competing against their colleagues (friends) for a limited number of roles
- Being put on a redeployment list and receiving notifications of roles that bear no resemblance to their strengths or ambitions
- Formal consultation processes with scripted conversations and stock answers to questions
- Working your notice period knowing that there's work to be done when you're gone that no one has the capacity or the skills to do
- Being put on gardening leave, stuck in-between the past and the future
- Accepting a new role in the organization and it's not as expected

Even if your organization runs restructuring processes in the best possible way, it's still tough. There is perhaps one exception: if you were going to leave anyway.

Change challenge: Redundancies

If your role is made redundant at any point in your career, the experience can take an emotional toll. Although what's happening is that the role you are in is being made redundant, it's almost impossible to avoid the feeling that it's personal, that you as a person are being made redundant. Redundancy sets internal alarm bells ringing. Being rejected by your workplace, losing your colleagues, and no longer being connected to how you often describe yourself is hard. The idea that you must go and search for a new role and face being rejected again can trigger your survival warning system. This is not a great place from which to put your best foot forward, to step into a job search, or to give your best performance at an interview. Even if your role survived the process, you'll likely be losing colleagues, your role will be different, and you may find that the trust you once had of your organization is a little tarnished by the process.

Change challenge: Exhaustion

Due to the rate and regularity of change, many people are struggling with change exhaustion.[40] One change follows another, with multiple processes overlapping, people exiting the business and new people starting. It may seem like the only solution to being caught in a change storm is to leave and go somewhere with calmer winds. Yet there are very few places left that aren't experiencing enormous amounts of change. Every industry is being disrupted. It's not always about escaping from the storm, it's learning how to ride the winds and use their energy to propel you forward – inside or outside the organization.

[40] M.W. Duffy and L. Fosslien, *Managers, what are you doing about change exhaustion?* Harvard Business Review (4 May 2022). Available from: https://hbr.org/2022/05/managers-what-are-you-doing-about-change-exhaustion [accessed 7 September 2022].

Reframing to redirection

Dragging us back from the dark side of change, it's not all bad or always bad. Change brings about the opportunity for career moves, to build new skills and work in new ways. Perhaps it's that nudge to step out of your comfort zone, encouraging you to do something positive about your career? It's very difficult to see a redirection as it's happening, it's best seen via the rear-view mirror once the dust has settled. Looking back, you'll be able to put the pieces together and see the bigger picture. Working through it feels at best uncomfortably exciting and at worst totally terrifying. When you're facing a redirection, you may need an injection of courage to help you step out of your comfort zone and walk towards the new opportunity.

Never attempt to go through any change challenge alone. This is the time to assemble your **Squad** (see chapter 7), openly ask for help, and utilize the ideas, connections, and contacts these wonderful humans offer. This is the moment when all that investment in those relationships pays off.

 WorkJoy story – Restructures to redirection

After my early career as a lawyer, I had been working in a large organization for more than 10 years, in senior corporate governance and risk roles. The business had been going through regular reorganizations and, although my role had survived the changes, it felt like we were becoming more siloed. Through each change, my role expanded, but it seemed to just be more of the same type of work, without that feeling of development or growth. I was starting to feel stuck and had a gloomy cloud over me, yet I didn't know what I wanted

or what I could do about it. I used the WorkJoy toolkit to help me get under the skin of where the cracks were. I embarked on a mission to reconnect with my role and organization. I stepped out of my comfort zone and showed my leadership skills by presenting to the Executive Team. I talked openly to my manager about wanting to do more in leading people. And, most importantly, I worked on myself.

I re-wrote the stories I had been telling myself about not being brave by reminding myself of all the courageous moves I have made in my life. I connected with my values and how passionate I am about leading people. I realized that I had the potential to add my skills to any organization. I remembered how important learning and growth within my job is to me. This process took me from being caught in the fog of gloom to having a sense of self-belief and clarity on what I wanted next.

When the next round of restructures headed my way, I was able to make the choices that were right for me. I was approached early on to discuss an alternative role within the organization. This position felt 'safe' and a continuation of what I had already been doing throughout my career, albeit in a slightly different setting. As a naturally risk-averse person, this is the sort of opportunity I would have previously pushed hard to get, to reassure myself I still had a role to play in the organization. But I knew deep down this role wouldn't move me towards my goals and it wouldn't bring me joy or help me grow. So, I engaged my courage, and chose redundancy. I wasn't in control of the situation; I was in control of the choices I made. It was a big decision, yet I knew it was right for me. My next challenge is finding a role and an organization where I can utilize my skills and feel that sense of growth!

Wrong-sized jobs

This one is a source of much WorkGloom and can lead to the life-takeover effect if left unchecked. People are notoriously bad at defining the right size and shape of jobs. They will advertise a role as being their standard 37 hours a week, yet that job may take only 20 hours, or (more often than that) 55! Most of the time, this is not a deliberate act of malice as it is quite a hard thing to estimate. Different people take different lengths of time to complete tasks and many jobs are no longer about how many things it is reasonable to ask someone to produce in a day or how many bits of data can be put into a log. They are more about what goes on in your minds, how you connect the dots, create solutions, and make decisions. Could you tell me now how long it would take you to create a solution for a client's special request? Probably not. Best guess is all they have. Where organizations get it wrong is doubling down on their guess work and insisting a job can be done within a certain time frame when all the evidence points in the other direction.

If you find yourself in this position, it's time to have a conversation with your **Boss** (chapter 10) and work out what's realistic and what the route to making it 'right sized' is. You may also want to consider which **Boundaries** (chapter 4) are important to implement.

Scope creep

This one can be a source of WorkJoy or WorkGloom depending on which way the creep is directed! It's not unreasonable to expect that the job you do will match the job description, yet it could be an unrealistic one. Job descriptions are like a wish list, representing everything a manager can think of that is required to be done. Often, they are written based on what the previous incumbent did in the role – so it's born out of their skills and strengths. If it's a new role, it's formed in the imagination of the creator – never translated into the practical reality. Even if you manage to start on script, it's highly likely you won't stay there. What is a priority one week may have morphed into a whole new area by the following month. This may mean stepping out of your comfort zone – learning different parts of the business, expanding your skill set, and broadening your horizons and potential career opportunities. It can be brilliant. It doesn't always work in that direction though and it can move you backwards, getting stuck into the grind or the detail, when you want to be on the strategy, or doing a job you moved on from years ago. These things can be acceptable in the short term, but if the scope realigns to be all of this, all the time, some serious consideration needs to be given to whether the role, in its new format, is what you really want.

If you've found yourself in a role that is creeping in the wrong direction, it's time to have a conversation with your **Boss** (chapter 10) about if/when you'll get back on track. If it's creeping in the right direction, embrace it, and see where it leads your career.

Fake promotions

This causes mixed emotions and can be a real gnarly issue to resolve – turning it from potentially joyful to gloomy. Not all career moves fit into the promotions category, yet when they happen, they can affirm your growth. When they come with the badges that prove the promotion, like job title changes and reward, that makes the promotion feel real. There are many occasions, however, when organizations use fake promotions, like when someone leaves and suddenly you get the pleasure of taking on their workload for no additional reward. The organization saves that person's entire salary, and you get double the workload. Or when there's a big project and your boss says, 'this will be great for your profile in the organization'. You're up for some career development so you take on the challenge of the project, you work your socks off, and then there's no longer an end date, it's now business as usual. This is one to balance as taking on extra projects, showing what you can do beyond your core role and being open to development can be a source of WorkJoy and can be great for your career. The key is to know when it's genuine, understand where and how this will enable your development, and be clear about what the expectations are. Again, it's an open conversation to have with your boss. Tread carefully, as you don't want the opportunity to disappear.

Imbalanced loyalty

A giant source of WorkGloom is the impact of imbalanced loyalty. Spend a moment and consider what sacrifices you make on the organization's behalf – unpaid overtime, the giving of yourself, your knowledge, and your skills. Perhaps remember the times you chose to stay when you could have left. Maybe you stayed out of loyalty to your team, your customers, or even your manager? Yet, if the organization was going through change and your role was on a list, would your organization offer you the same amount of loyalty as you've shown them? Or would they go ahead and make your role redundant? The point here isn't about having no loyalty. It's remembering that an organization isn't a person, it doesn't feel the same way, it can't – you're married to the equivalent of a robot, not a human.

 Reflection questions

- What are you offering your organization in terms of loyalty?
- What are you getting in return?
- Do you feel that it's balanced?

The trick here is to have enough loyalty, not too much and not too little. Engage yourself with your work, get involved in your organization. Don't sacrifice too much of you, or your life, for it. Keep the perspective that there is no such thing as a job for life. Your loyalty to the organization (not the people within it) should only be equal to the length of any severance package and notice period you may be entitled to if they press the go button.

Square peg – round hole

Your human need to belong applies at work, with a desire to be valued and respected for being yourself, and not just for the work you do. Sometimes it just feels right. Sometimes it feels right in your immediate team, but not beyond it, or vice versa. Sometimes you may feel like a square peg in a round hole. In this situation, you may try to adjust yourself to fit in, shaving the edges, squishing into uncomfortable spaces, and attempting to change who you are. This rarely leads to joy. It's almost impossible to move anywhere upwards from neutral if you must constantly adjust. A feeling of lack of belonging can stem from different reasons, including being somehow different from the archetype of most people you work with. This can range from demographic factors like race, gender, and disability to style factors like levels of introversion and extroversion and levels of creativity. There is a big difference from being respected for what difference you bring and being excluded because of your difference. The first is progressive and how organizations will leverage diversity to achieve better outcomes. This is where the hole is changing shape to fit your square peg (a hexagon holds a square nicely) not the other way around. The second is toxic and, unless the organization goes on a major transformation, it's unlikely to change.

Reflection questions

- How included do you feel at work?
- Are you valued for being yourself or are you getting bent out of shape?

Only you will know the level of belonging that you need to create WorkJoy. If you're getting WorkGloom from a lack of it, and you're not seeing any progress made (remember progress over perfection) it may be time to seek out somewhere new.

Is this organization right for you?

How do you know whether to stay in an organization and when to leave? The answer is nearly always 'it depends!'. You may decide to stay when all around you decide to move or vice versa. You have choices to make, and you will never know in advance if the choice you make is the 'right' one. You can only go on the information you have at the time. Let both facts and feelings guide you.

- Facts offer perspective and help you navigate your path.
- Feelings allow you to connect with, understand, and seek out the joy, whether you stay or go.

Deciding to stay

There are some obvious things that would lead to a 'I want to stay' answer that usually come from the more joyful end of the spectrum. Like when the work you do is interesting and engaging, when the relationship with your boss and your team is firing on all cylinders, and when your organization aligns to your **Values** (see chapter 3) and demonstrates how it values you. If you feel like you're growing and that there's opportunity in the future. There are a few watch-outs in this zone. The first is getting too comfortable and not noticing the changes until you're behind the times – in your career, in how you do things – and your progress stalls. There are also practical considerations like location and working hours, benefits, friendships at work, and all the stuff and things that make a difference in your life. The key here is understanding that you are making a choice to stay for those reasons, even if there are other things that bring you gloom.

Deciding to go

There are some obvious things that would lead to a 'I want to go' answer that usually come from gloomy end of the spectrum. Like when you've fallen out of love with the work, when the relationship with your boss has entered the irreconcilable differences category, or when your organization no longer seems to align with your values. In stark contrast, new organizations can twinkle from a distant view, luring you towards a seemingly perfect world. There is no such thing as a 'perfect' organization, so sometimes it may be safer to stick with what you know. Doing your research on whether you want to or can fall (back) in love with your organization before you start divorce proceedings will stand you in good stead. Even if the answer is still 'get me out of here!' after trying, you'll be doing it from a better-informed place of perspective rather than running for the hills. It can also help you have a joyful exit.

Love the one you're with

Your level of love for your organization can range from the rose-tinted spectacled, totally besotted throws of passion (the honeymoon period), to the 'I know you by heart' phase where everything is in flow, to the 'better the devil you know' when the reality comes into view and of course the 'I wish I never have to see you again' of the impending break up. These can apply to the different types of work relationships – the possibilities are almost endless. You could be feeling wonderful about your team yet feeling unconnected with this work itself. Perhaps you're ready to break up with the organization yet you're loving your customers. Maybe your organization does inspirational work that you love, yet the team isn't quite your cup of tea.

Whether it's a small niggle or you're heading towards a separation it can help to remind yourself why you decided to hook up with this job in the first place. At some point you went from casually dating (applying for it), chose to move in together (interview process), and got hitched (contract signing). There must have been a reason you wanted to work at this organization. Even if it was a 'you'll do for now', reconnect with what it was, then ask yourself:

Reflection questions

- Have you lost sight of that connection and it just needs sewing back together?
- Has it been lost over time or through change?
- Does that reason no longer serve you as it once did?

Reconnecting with your organization

Here are three experiments you can try out to seek out reconnection with your organization.

1. Go on a first date

Sometimes you're just a bit bored and not seeing the great things your organization has to offer. To combat the drudge, try going on a new first date with your work.

- Dive deeper into your projects
- Get to know your team better
- Seek out what's going on in the far-flung reaches of your organization.

Have a poke around the nooks and crannies and see what you might find.

 Reflection questions

- Did you find anything unexpected or exciting?
- Is there genuinely nothing left to explore?
- Or has the relationship run its course?

2. Put on your rose-tinted spectacles

Choose to put on your rose-tinted spectacles for a while. Spend some time focusing on the good stuff and working out where the joy comes from.

 Reflection questions

- Could building an even stronger relationship with the good stuff outweigh the 'it's complicated' areas?
- Would a little extra effort in a challenging area go a long way?
- Or are the rose-tinted spectacles not strong enough to deal with the darkness?

3. Go on a work safari

Get your exploration kit on and look beyond your current role, team, and context.

Allow yourself to explore new roles, teams, and organizations to see how a new or different relationship might fit.

- Explore the different elements and functions of your business
- Enlist tour guides from different areas and seek out feedback from the locals
- Consider the good, the bad, and the ugly

 Reflection questions

- Is the grass greener on the other side or is it a mirage?
- Or is it a tatty old town for you now?

Even if there is no such thing as a perfect job, team, or organization, you can craft a working world that fits you well. A world where you can enjoy spending your time and where you are able to negate the little niggles – because overall, you're comfy together. Maybe it's not a forever thing. Maybe it's right for right now.

Joyful goodbye

Always aim to leave an organization on good terms and avoid burning any bridges. You never know when you may want to boomerang back into that organization, or who might want to hire you again when they move on. The people you've worked with previously are often those that offer or connect you to a future career move. The minimum standard for leaving well is to be professional. The maximum is leaving as an advocate. Sending gratitude emails to those who have supported you and shouting about what a great time you've had to your replacement is advocacy. As is recommending it as a great place to work on LinkedIn or Glassdoor. Even if you've not made the decision to leave yourself, it doesn't negate the entire experience you had with that organization. If it was great for 10 years until you were made redundant, the 10 years haven't been wiped out by that one thing (even though it was a big thing!).

Of course, a 'high' might not always be possible. Leaving with a stroppy attitude, by sharing sensitive information, by slagging off people or writing a strongly worded exit email with all the unresolved gripes you hold will not entice people to consider you again in the future. That's burning the house down as you leave. Always remember other people must still live in that house, so don't leave it full of smoke for them to choke on. Adding extra fuel to the gloom isn't very helpful.

Leaving badly, if done publicly or identifiably, can give any employers you want to work for pause to consider if you are a difficult person. That bitterness, even if it was caused by an organization that didn't do its best for you, is in no way attractive to a future employer. It will put them off hiring you and if you carry that bad feeling with you, it will taint any interviews or probation periods. You will get labelled as miserable – full of gloom. People are attracted to joy, so choose your attitude carefully.

The route to WorkJoy – Organizations

Using the active WorkJoy formula, let's explore some ideas of how you could use the three Es of Engagement, Energy, and Experimentation within the context of **Organizations** to both cultivate WorkJoy and reframe WorkGloom.

Organizations	Cultivating WorkJoy	Reframing WorkGloom
Engagement	Notice all the different ways your organization brings you joy, so you know where to focus your attention.	Remember that most people within the organizations you work for are trying their best and that there is no such thing as the perfect organization.
Energy	Invest your energy in seeking out more of the things about the organization that bring you joy (e.g., if it's about the people, join a networking group, or if it's about the customers, get more connected with their needs).	Reframe the choices you are making about where you invest your energy (e.g., if it's not the right organization for you, invest in finding the right place for you rather than being gloomy about where you are right now).
Experimentation	Experiment with developing solutions to the organizational issues you observe (e.g., getting involved in employee focus groups or volunteering to be part of improvement project teams).	Try out the first dates, work safari, and rose-tinted spectacles experiments to reconnect with your organization (and discover hidden opportunities for joy!).

Now that you've explored WorkJoy from the perspective of **Organizations,** let's consider a key feature within all of them, the people who lead and manage you, your **Bosses.**

CHAPTER 10

BOSSES

Introduction

Whether you call them managers, team leaders, heads of, directors, leaders, or supervisors, nearly everyone has a boss of some kind. If you're an entrepreneur, your boss may come in an alternate form, like investors or clients. When they're the right boss for you, they can be the bringers of immense joy, enabling you to thrive. If they're not, they can be the harbingers of gloom. In my experience working with hundreds of leaders, 99% of them are working their socks off to do a good job, attempting to balance the needs of the business with your needs. In this chapter, you'll focus on the boss closest to you (a line manager/supervisor) and consider what to do if you're with the wrong boss and how to spot a great one. You'll also turn the tables and explore how to be a great bossee (yes, that's an invented word!).

The reality of bosses

Being a boss is not an easy gig. Some people take to it like a duck to water, many find it a struggle. Organizational structures often mean it's hard to move up the ranks without being a manager, so there's a lot of people who've become managers by career necessity rather than having a particular penchant for it. It's part of a boss's job to make tough decisions. They may find these uncomfortable, or even agonize over them. Sometimes, they must do what they've been instructed to do by their bosses (who were told by their bosses, etc.). They might have to dismiss your best work buddy because, as much as you love working with them, they're not that good at their job. Maybe they need to restructure the team to meet the changing needs of the business and that impacts on you. Perhaps they need to bring in a new layer of management because their role has expanded too much and now you report to someone new. Maybe they've had to stop spending as much time supporting and mentoring you because you've made it and there is someone else more in need of their attention.

This stuff happens, it's the reality of the modern workplace. Some of the things that bosses do that bring some gloom may be exactly what they need to do to fulfil their role. It doesn't mean they don't care; it means they're doing hard things.

The myth of management

It's tempting to believe in a mythical leader who rises beyond the echelons of humanity, always gets it right, and can magically solve your problems. Yet all leaders and managers are mere mortals. Whatever type of boss you have, whether they're brand new to leadership or someone with significant experience, if they're an expert in your subject matter or have no idea what you do, by the nature of their role, they will influence your working life.

For the sake of simplicity, let's put bosses into three categories:

- Hellish bosses
- Hero bosses
- Human bosses

Hellish bosses

A truly awful boss can make everything at work seem gloomy. They fill you with fear and insecurity, and make you dread your working days. Their presence makes you shudder, an email from them gets your anxiety rising and if they say 'we need to talk' you consider running for the hills. They are the ones that:

1. Have no interest in your life beyond work
2. Are focused on your inputs (hours in the office/online)
3. Micro-manage your every move
4. Have favourites and enemies
5. Dismiss your ideas
6. Bark orders at you
7. Move goal posts so you never know where you stand
8. Berate you if you make a mistake
9. Blame you when things go wrong
10. Fail to recognize the things you do well

These types of bosses exist in the extreme version, where all 10 of these characteristics come out to play, all the time. It's almost impossible to live with this type of boss. It destroys your self-belief; your confidence will collapse, and you'll likely burn out. Perhaps, you'll be able to manage the situation, by trying to get in their good books. Then you realize they don't have good books and regardless of how hard you work, however much you adapt to their whims and whether you've given every single last drop of blood, sweat, and tears – you will never make them satisfied. It's just not possible.

These bosses also exist in a slightly milder version, they're hell-ish, with some of these characteristics coming out to play, some of the time. These behaviours squeeze out of the edges during challenging times. If you can work out the triggers, you might be able to manage around them. If they're seemingly random and you never quite know what you're going to get, it can be massively unsettling.

Hero bosses

A fantastic boss can make everything at work seem joyful. They inject you with the inspiration, confidence, and permission to make your working world a pleasure rather than a chore. They are the ones that:

1. Care about you as a person
2. Focus on your outputs (what you deliver and how you do it)
3. Are invested in your success and your career
4. Act with kindness when you need it
5. Push you to be better
6. Listen to you without judgement
7. Advise, guide, mentor, and coach you
8. Recognize when you do things well
9. Are clear about expectations and standards
10. Let you know when you are off course and help you correct

These bosses exist in their wonderful glory, but they are a rarely spotted beast. They exist in only a few natural habitats. You might find them in special places with brilliant development programmes or organizations that care deeply about people. They can also exist in the most barren of workplaces, where they've experienced the gloom themselves and have chosen not to pass it on, becoming little havens of happiness.

They also exist in a slightly less glorious form – a hero-ish version, with slightly less glitter – where they do most of these things, most of the time. At some point, however, they will inevitably fall short of the fantasy and fall off the pedestal. Beware the rose-tinted spectacles of hero worship. That is a standard that people can't maintain. Be a fan, sure, advocate for how great a boss they are, but always leave them room to be human.

 Reflection question

- What behaviours is your boss displaying regularly?

Human bosses

Bosses are humans. The reality is that most bosses are neither all hell-ish or all hero-ish and they're unlikely to be at one or other end of the spectrum all the time. It's unrealistic to expect 100% performance, 24/7, from even the most progressive of bosses. In real life, human bosses:

1. Are vulnerable and struggle too – they did not become immune to work and life-based challenges when they got their boss title
2. Experience the challenges of working life and often take on what their teams are challenged with too
3. Feel joy and gloom just like everyone else and try to do their best

4. Have the good, bad, and ugly days just like the rest of us
5. Slip up and say or do the wrong things, even when they're trying hard to get it right
6. Get mad and throw their toys out of the pram, have a strop, or a little cry when it gets too much
7. Forget to say thank you sometimes, even though they're really, truly grateful to have you in their team
8. Are trying to balance the needs of many and can't please everyone all the time
9. Often must act as piggy in the middle between their direct reports and their bosses
10. Are trying to make it through the day, as well as they possibly can whilst riding a unicycle and juggling fireballs

Realign your expectations

When you look upwards, are you seeking perfection, wanting your role models to be superheroes? Whether they're your line manager or the most senior people in your organization, do you want more from them than they can realistically give? If you want to feel more joy when it comes to your bosses, you'll need to adjust your expectations. You must leave room for their humanity. Consider these questions to uncover your expectations.

 WorkJoy WorkBook

You can access the Realigning Your Expectations of Your Boss template in the WorkJoy WorkBook

 Reflection questions

- What are your expectations of your boss/es?
- Are those expectations based in fantasy or reality?

WorkJoy story – Being a boss

I was promoted to an HR manager role following a restructure. It was a brand-new role and a brand-new team. I went from line managing one person to seven and, although I knew them from across the business, I'd never worked with any of them before and we were all thrown together into unknown territory. It was my job to figure everything out! I felt real anxiety about what the team's remit would be, what my remit would be, and what my responsibilities were as a manager. I'd had some amazing, really supportive managers before, and I felt like I wasn't them.

My approach was to strip things right back. I figured that, in order to enjoy what I'm doing, I needed to be patient in learning what my team does and how we could improve processes. I knew I couldn't just sit in an ivory tower and tell people what to do. Gradually, I became more confident in asking questions of my team, and in not feeling that I needed to know the answers. Then my manager left, and it was expected that myself and another manager would take the helm. Neither of us wanted to do it, but I knew it would be good for my career.

The WorkJoy tools helped me to identify the impact I have on my team, department, and company. That was the lightbulb moment for me! The irony is that, to become a good boss, I had to overcome my self-limiting beliefs that I'm not a good boss. I've learned that I don't have to be the bosses I've had before. I just need to be me.

Who's in charge?

It's likely that your boss has some control over the work that you do. That control could range from total autonomy to slight influence. One thing they are never totally in control of is your WorkJoy. They oversee their own WorkJoy, not yours. Of course, they have influence, yet it is only you who can be fully responsible for your joy – in work and beyond.

The wrong boss

If you're struggling with a boss who isn't right for you, avoid calling them a bad boss. It could just be a personality clash; not everyone gets along with everyone else. Perhaps reframe them as a boss who doesn't get the best out of you. If your boss is bringing you immense gloom, yet you're not doing anything to change the situation, then that's on you. If you find yourself in a wrong boss situation, ask yourself these questions:

 Reflection questions
Have you...

- Sought out ways to manage their impact on you?
- Shared feedback with them?
- Reported poor behaviour through the appropriate channels?
- Sought out a different role inside your organization?
- Started the process of seeking a new role in a new organization?

This is not to say that sharing your feedback or reporting poor behaviour will be a solution, yet it is better than passively accepting the situation. If you have not taken any steps to make things better, it is unlikely their behaviours will miraculously change. If you choose to take no action, you are choosing to live in the gloom. If there are other reasons why you're staying and putting up with the wrong boss (maybe you love the organization, or the team is amazing) be clear that you've weighed up your options and are now deliberately keeping yourself in the lion's den.

Moan and move on

Having an occasional moan about your boss can be cathartic and may help you work your way out of a mild case of gloom. Try to have it with a trusted squaddie (see chapter 7) who can give you a balanced perspective and rounded advice. This usually means chatting with someone who is outside of your team, to get unbiased advice. Once you've let the moan out, it's time to move on.

Another option is to put pen to paper and get writing. Put it all down in a letter, every single gripe, everything that made you angry, every error made. Then *don't send it*. Keep it if you must – but only to remind you what brings you gloom so that you can know what you are looking for in a future organization. Or to remind yourself how far you've moved on. Or to go back and laugh about how seriously you took everything back then when you didn't know better. Even better, chop it up, shred it – and let it go (see the conclusion – **Choices**).

How to spot a good boss

Always seek out a boss who sits somewhere between human and hero. A person who spends 70%–80% of their time right of the centre line. Allow them the space to cross to the dark side occasionally. Don't judge them for it, support them back into the light. Make sure they're the kind of person who is self-aware enough to know that they crossed the line and have enough self-esteem to say they got it wrong.

A good boss will:

1. Be open about what their strengths are and where their passions lie
2. Tell you what they're not good at and feel comfy asking for help
3. Give you clarity on their expectations

4. Share enough of themselves beyond work that you feel connected to them personally as well as professionally
5. Know they're wonderfully imperfect and embrace this openly
6. Pick up the phone and say, 'tell me what I can do to help' (or even better, just do something that is helpful) when you're in a crisis
7. Muck in to support and help create the fix when it all goes wrong
8. Tell you when you've done something brilliantly
9. Give you direct feedback when you need to improve
10. Invest in your personal and professional development

Whenever you're seeking a new or different role, put as much energy into discovering and assessing who your boss (or bosses) will be as you do into considering and analysing the job content, reward, and growth. A boss can make or break your day – choose wisely!

If you're working with a great boss, make sure they know it! As people work their way through the leadership ranks, they get less and less feedback on their performance. Be the person who tells them what they're great at, and what they can do even more of. They will be grateful for your candour.

Being a good bossee…

Have you ever considered how you're doing as one of your boss's team members, as a bossee? The boss/employee relationship is a two-way street, yet it's easy to focus on how their behaviour impacts on you rather than looking at how you impact them. If you both know how your behaviour contributes to each other's WorkJoy or WorkGloom and do your best to work with that information, you'll be set up for a more meaningful relationship. This could range from the micro-moments (like grabbing them a coffee when they're snowed under) to stepping in to support them with a big work challenge. If you can, develop a relationship where you know each other well enough to spot opportunities to bring a little joy (or ward off some gloom). The investment of your energy here will pay off. Here are some examples:

	Joy	Gloom
Your boss	If their joy comes from observing you doing well, have you told them about your latest successes?	If their gloom comes from back-to-back meetings, have you offered to sub yourself into some of them?
You	If your joy comes from being challenged, have you asked them for their thoughts on what you could do differently?	If your gloom comes from a difficult relationship with a client, have you asked for their advice on how to handle it?

 Reflection questions

- What are your boss's expectations of you?
- What are you doing to help them to help you? (e.g., telling them what you need)
- How could you bring a little WorkJoy to them today?

Buddy to boss, mate to manager

One of the most awkward and angst-inducing career moments can happen when:

- You get promoted and you're now your buddy's boss
- Your mate gets promoted and they're now your manager

This change of role will change the dynamic of your relationship. If you become responsible for your friend's work performance and for their productivity, the types of conversation you will need to have will change. If your mate now holds in their hands the keys that open doors to your development and growth, that's going to change the game. If you're ever in this situation (on either side), instead of ignoring it, work through the awkward feeling and have a direct conversation. Accept that things will have to change. Your friendship will be different. Your working relationship will be charting a new course.

Here are some starter questions:

- What does this new dynamic mean for our friendship?
- What does this new role mean for our working relationship?
- What new boundaries do we need to put in place?
- What do we need to say goodbye to?

The route to WorkJoy – Bosses

Using the active WorkJoy formula, let's explore some ideas of how you could use the three Es of Engagement, Energy, and Experimentation within the context of **Bosses** to both cultivate WorkJoy and reframe WorkGloom.

Bosses	Cultivating WorkJoy	Reframing WorkGloom
Engagement	Notice all the great things your boss does for you and share your gratitude for these things (this will help them do more of it!).	Engage your thinking towards your boss having influence rather than control; you have choices about who you work with.
Energy	Invest your energy in understanding your boss's expectations of you, so that you know where you stand (e.g., ask directly and check in regularly – don't wait for an annual performance review!)	Define what type of manager brings the best out of you and invest your energy in helping your current boss help you or finding a new boss who better caters to your needs
Experimentation	Experiment with being a good bossee. Find ways to support them by offering your services (e.g., if they are struggling with a task, ask what you can do to help or if they're not great at a task that you're great at/want to develop in, offer to take it off their hands).	Reframe the notion that brilliant bosses are perfect. Experiment with giving your boss space to be human. Try filling any gaps with support from your **Squad** instead (e.g., if they're not a great mentor, someone from your squad will be).

Now that you've explored who's in your **Squad,** the shape of your **Career,** the **Organization** you work with, and the impact of your **Boss,** let's move to the final part and work on making WorkJoy happen. You're now going to focus on how to set and go get your **Goals.**

PART 4

MAKING IT HAPPEN

CHAPTER 11

GOALS

Introduction

Now that you've explored the inner and outer WorkJoy factors, let's look at making great things happen by setting goals and taking purposeful action (remember WorkJoy is an active pursuit!). Goals can be tricky things, often hard to define and sometimes challenging to see through as real life gets in the way. I've had my fair share of goals end up in the bin, and rather than the joy of achievement, I've ended up feeling like my progress has stalled. In this chapter, you'll set your sights on goals that really matter to you (using my PROUD framework which has worked wonders for me!) and plan a route to get you where you want to go. You'll also explore the hurdles that might get in your way and how your habits could make or break your mission. Let's start by contemplating different types of goals.

Types of goals

The feeling of achieving a goal is a core source of WorkJoy for many people. That podium giving a sense of achievement. If you consider the setting of goals and the getting of goals, there is joy to be had along the way, not just at the end point. If you're mindful about your goals and you don't get first prize, you will still have found the joy in the journey. You already have goals, though whether you've defined them is a different question. Perhaps you're working towards something defined by someone else like work-based objectives, OKRs (objectives and key results) or KPIs (key performance indicators). The goals you set for yourself may be languishing, not fully explored.

Sometimes goals are the daydream type, akin to the 'if I win the lottery' conversations. Although they may be the fantasy, they are worth indulging in, to explore that version of what you want in your life, without any limitations. Then there's the grandly stated, New-Year's-resolution-type goals. These goals often have a health or wellbeing slant to them (created amidst the food coma of festive over-indulging). They're the ones that have your full energy to start with, yet by 17 January when it's raining and dark at 6am, your 'I'm going to cycle to work every single day' goal has been thrown in the bin.

You may have goals that you think you should work towards, because your education, society, or traditions have been convincing you where you 'should' be 'by now' on the standard path. From work, to relationships, to families, to how much you should be earning and what type of holidays you go on. These societal 'norms' drive us subconsciously, even if they're not the path you would choose for yourself. These 'should goals' are often unhelpful, as they're chasing other people's dreams. If you're should-ing all over yourself it's probably time to re-think, re-craft, and re-define the goals that matter to you.

Goals are about change

At the heart of a goal is a desire to change. Whether that's reforming habits, building a new skill, or achieving an outcome. It's the process of going from one state and into a new one. Before you even consider what the goal itself is, it can be helpful to consider two things:

- The level of change desired (from minor to major)
- The level of energy you are prepared to put into making the change happen

Consider these four types of goal that relate the level of the three Es you need to make them happen and the level of desired change:

Resolutions	Revolution
• Steadfast and inflexible • Often from the 'should' bucket • Likelihood of long-term change minimal	• Big change • Can be enforced or chosen • Focus on speed • Will be hard work
Revelation	**Evolution**
• Change in thinking or mindset • Requires little action • Change is likely to be in your approach rather than the outcome	• Minor to major change • Broken into small actions over time • Focus on growth • Can be flexed to fit real life

Reflection questions

- What types of goal have you set previously?
- How did they work for you?
- What type of goal might you want to focus your attention on next?

Goal setting

To be able to get your goals, it helps to set them well, and your upfront investment will equal better outcomes and a more enjoyable expedition. By this point in your WorkJoy adventure, you'll likely have some thoughts about where you want to focus your attention and experience some change. Keep this in mind as you work through the PROUD assessment – checking and challenging if you really want it.

WorkJoy WorkBook

Head to the WorkJoy WorkBook for the Goal Setting template

The PROUD assessment

Take an idea you feel strongly about that you'd like to flesh out in more detail. With this idea, work through the reflection questions from the PROUD list below.

PROUD	Reflection questions
Purpose and passion	• What is the purpose of the goal? • How does it link to your bigger plans, your **Life** (see chapter 2) and your **Values** (see chapter 3) • Does it align to your passion, the things you love to do and that bring you joy inside and outside of work?

Revolutionary and realistic	• What change is going to come when you achieve this goal? • How will that change influence your life and your work? • Is the goal a daydream or is there some reality to it? • Have you shrunk it too much because it's too big or too far from reach? Have you made it so big you feel it's impossible?
Opportunity and options	• What opportunities, resources, and people are out there to help you along the way? (chapter 7) • How could you seek these things out? • What are the different routes and options for you now? • How could you decide which route to try first? • What about option B, C, D?
Unique and uplifting	• What is it about the goal that is personal for you? (as opposed to tagging along with someone else's goal or taking an opinion on what you should do as instruction) • Does the idea of working on the goal light you up? • Can you feel the desire to make it happen growing?
Destination and determination	• What will be different in your world – both when you've achieved it and in the steps along the way? • What are you prepared to put in to make it happen? (active WorkJoy formula – see chapter 1) • What might you need to **Learn** and develop? (chapter 6) • What **Boundaries** might you need to set or adapt to make it happen? (chapter 4)

Once you have considered the questions below, ask yourself 'is this a goal I am serious about pursuing?' If the answer's *no*, pick something else you're interested in and work through the steps again. This process will help you rule out goals that aren't what you really want! If it's a resounding *yes* – get it defined!

Crafting your goal

According to research by Dr Gail Matthews,[41] you are more likely to achieve a goal by writing it down. Make sure it's:

- **Simple** – anyone should be able to read it and know what you're aiming to do
- **Positive** – what you want the outcome to be rather than what you want to move away from
- **Timed** – a deadline or milestone for next action will help to focus the mind

If you're feeling creative, drawing or painting goals can be inspirational, as can creating poems or little ditties about them. Once your work of art is crafted, put it somewhere you will see it every day (front of a notebook, your desktop, or your fridge door) so that it stays front of mind. You'll be amazed how many wonderful things seem to happen when you purposefully set your intention and allow your subconscious to do the work.

Goal getting

Living in the real world, you know that there are things that get in your way, thwarting your progress. Pre-empting

---

[41] A. Feinstein, *Why you should be writing down your goals*. Forbes (8 April 2014). Available from: www.forbes.com/sites/ellevate/2014/04/08/why-you-should-be-writing-down-your-goals/?sh=390f0cd3397c [accessed 7 September 2022].

some of the hurdles may help you to find ways to work around these challenges. Other hurdles may be totally unpredictable, a side swipe that you couldn't prepare for. Trying to prepare for those is a fool's errand, so let's focus on what you know may get in your way.

 Reflection questions

- What can you envisage getting in your way?
- How might these things impact you achieving your goal?
  - Will they make it harder?
  - Might it take longer?
  - Could they totally derail you?
- When might these things crop up?
  - Is it a timing thing?
  - Is it situational?
- Who is in control of these things?
  - Other people?
  - You?
- Which hurdles are genuine issues and which hurdles have you put up for yourself?

For the genuine issues, those practical or logistical challenges, there is often a simple or obvious solution to work through. Perhaps you need to engage some supporters from your **Squad** (see chapter 7) to help work through them – it's so much better when working through problems together. The challenges that may be harder to overcome are those hurdles in your mind.

Limiting beliefs

So often, it is your own limiting beliefs and not a practical issue or situation that really get in your way. Much of your thinking is driven by your experiences, your fears, and your unhelpful **Stories** (see chapter 5) that tell us that everyone else is awesome and you're just faking it. To get a grip on some of your limiting beliefs, try completing these sentences:

When you're at your **best**, feeling brilliant, supported, and demonstrating your capability – the stories you tell yourself are…	When you're at your **middle** ground, feeling fine, pootling along, and doing okay – the stories you tell yourself are…	When you're at your **worst**, feeling insecure, unsure, unsupported, and lacking confidence – the stories you tell yourself are…
e.g., I am strong, I am capable, I'm great at…, I can do anything I put my mind to…	e.g., I'm pretty good at…, I know I can cope, I've been through challenges before…	e.g., everyone else is better than me, I am not good enough, people will laugh at me…

WorkJoy WorkBook

A template for the Limiting Beliefs Exercise is available in the WorkJoy WorkBook

It's likely you'll notice some limiting beliefs. Some of these may come from the 'when I'm at my worst' category but watch out for the 'when I'm at my best' category too. Both ends of the spectrum can have us out of kilter with reality!

The power of yet

Dr Carol Dweck[42] suggests that a solution to being stuck in a fixed mindset, with limiting beliefs, is to add the word *yet*

---

[42] C.S. Dweck, *Mindset: Changing the way you think to fulfil your potential* (2017).

to a sentence. The yet allows you to open your thinking to future possibilities even if it seems impossible now. The yet has power to move you towards action. Try this five-step approach to help you move from a limiting belief to a more joyful place, where you have created an integrated habit.

Five steps to bust a limiting belief

Steps	Example
Step 1: Limiting belief	I'm too busy to fit learning into my life
Step 2: The power of *yet*	I haven't found ways to fit learning into my life *yet*
Step 3: Move towards action	I am experimenting with how I fit learning into my life
Step 4: Recognizing learning	I have found ways to fit learning into my life
Step 5: Integrated habit	Learning is part of my life

 Reflection questions

- What limiting beliefs would you like to bust?
- How could you use *yet* to help you move to a more purposeful place?

Step 5 is the goal and to get there, you'll need to work out and work on your habits.

 WorkJoy WorkBook

A template for the Five Steps to Bust a Limiting Belief is available in the WorkJoy WorkBook

WorkJoy story – Using the power of yet

I'm a nurse specialist in the NHS. During the pandemic everything changed for me, I was redeployed to a more clinical area, and it all felt very chaotic. When things normalized, I felt like I didn't know who I was at work anymore. I'd lost my way. I had the opportunity to move from a Band 6 to a Band 7 role but didn't know how to establish myself as the senior person in the team. My goal was to get back in the zone of my work identity.

The WorkJoy focus on growth mindset was really powerful for me. I saw how many excuses I was making for myself and worked through them. The job I came from had a difficult team dynamic and I felt I carried that with me into this role. So, I wrote a letter to my old managers then shredded it. I always forget about that because I've let it go. It's completely gone!

The best thing I learned was the word 'Yet'. This little word really empowered me to ask questions of senior staff members and consultants. It's not that I don't want to know something, it's that I haven't had the chance to learn it yet. It's become a key principle in my management style. Above our desk at work I wrote, 'Team, we don't know about this YET.' Now, we learn something new each week because we write it on the board. Something about the word just chills me out.

As time has passed, I've settled into the job. The WorkJoy strategies have made a massive difference to me, at work and at home – because that's a job as well.

Habits

Falling into habits is a normal process that your wonderful brain makes happen for efficiency, creating preprogrammed responses to situations. Unfortunately, not all habits are helpful, and some are damaging. If you can harness helpful habits, they can go a long way to helping you achieve your goals. Research suggests that it takes around 66 days to form a new habit, so it requires effort and time. It isn't easy as your habits become hardwired into your thinking and behaviours, acting as your brain's autopilot. Let's consider what your habits are and whether they are helpful or unhelpful. What counts as helpful or unhelpful will be personal to you and one person's helpful habit may be seen by someone else as unhelpful. Tune in to what is enabling you and what might be making things harder. Some examples to get you started:

Helpful habits	Unhelpful habits
• Going for a daily walk • Asking questions to get clarity • Investing in your squad • Learning something new every day • Reflecting on your day • Keeping a log of successes • Drinking water	• Stewing on past conversations • Working late • Worrying about the unknown • Binge watching TV • Procrastinating • Scrolling social media • Forgetting to fuel yourself

Take a moment to consider some habits that fit into your helpful or unhelpful buckets.

Reflection questions

- Which helpful habits are core to how you do things?
- What unhelpful habits would you like to change?
- Who helps or hinders you building or breaking habits?

Building helpful habits

With a new habit you want to build or do more of, try these four different ways of building.

Reduce the friction	Habit stacking
Find ways to make new habits easier to do. For example: • To build the habit of speaking up more in meetings, you could write down some questions before a meeting starts so that you don't have to create them on the spot. • To build the habit of going to the gym before starting work, you could put your sports clothes out the night before.	Utilize the helpful habits you already have by coupling them with the new thing you want to do. For example: • To build the habit of planning your day, you could stack it onto your morning coffee/tea routine. • To build the habit of mindfulness in the morning, you could stack it onto brushing your teeth.
Temptation bundling	**Habit directed**
Couple the instantly gratifying 'want to' activities with the 'need to' behaviour providing long-term benefits. For example: • To build the habit of focusing on getting the hard thing done, focus your attention on it whilst listening to your favourite playlist.	Move from being goal directed to being habit directed. For example: Instead of 'I want to build my knowledge of leadership', try 'I'll read a book/watch a TED talk for 30 minutes at 7pm every Wednesday'.

• To build a habit of eating healthily, allow yourself a Netflix binge combined with eating a healthy snack.	• Instead of 'I want to get fit, so I'll go to the gym', try 'when I wake up at 6.30am on Tuesdays and Thursdays, I'll go to the gym'.

Why not experiment with some of these habit hacks and see how they work for you?

Disrupting unhelpful habits

If hacking your habits helps to build helpful ones, what can you do with those pesky unhelpful habits that seem to be hardwired?! Here's a process to work through to help you work out why they're there and what to do about them!

 WorkJoy WorkBook

You can access the Habit Review template in the WorkJoy WorkBook

The NECTAR method

N	Notice	The first step is to notice your unhelpful habit, when it happens and how it shows itself • Also notice your reaction to this habit • Define it – give it a name • Then accept it for what it is and tell it you no longer need it!
E	Evaluate	Work out *why* this habit was built in the first place – perhaps it once served a purpose? • Evaluate what impact it has on you • Evaluate how it might act as a barrier to your future

C	Consider	Reflect on the stories you tell yourself about this habit and consider: • Where this has influenced your story so far • Other examples of where you've changed habits for inspiration • What your story might look like if it were no longer a habit • What helpful habits could replace this unhelpful one
T	Tactics	• Now think about your tactics for disrupting this pattern • Try out different things / different options • Ask your squad for ideas and suggestions
A	Adapt	• Start adapting to a new way of thinking and acting • If you try a tactic and it doesn't work, don't give up! Keep trying or try a different tactic • Acknowledge your progress (especially the small changes) and don't expect perfection – you're rewiring your brain – it's not easy
R	Repeat	• If at first you don't succeed, try, and try again • Repeat, adapt, repeat until rewiring is complete

Now that you've explored some of your unhelpful habits, let's work through two simple disruption tactics that may help you rewire your habits.

Before, during, after

Try moving the point at which you recognize you're doing the 'thing' (whatever it is you want to stop/change) earlier in the process:

- It usually starts at the **after** stage when you go 'oh no I did that again'. Reflect on these times when you notice them, run through the NECTAR process so that you understand the habit better.
- With practice you can start to be more aware of the habit and move to 'oh no, I'm *doing* that'. When you get to this **during** stage, acknowledge it – don't judge yourself for it. Explore the situation and circumstances that led to it happening.
- Over time and with more effort, you can move to 'ah-ha – I'm *about* to *do* that'. When you get to the **before** stage, you are more likely to be able to do something about it (although there's no guarantee you won't do it anyway!).

Stop, breathe, change

When you get to the **before** stage, try this to limit your likelihood of doing the 'thing':

- **Stop** – Stop whatever you're doing. Put your pen down, stop talking, stop moving.
- **Breathe** – There are very few situations where taking a few deep breaths won't help you.
- **Change** – Ask yourself some of these questions:
  - Is this what you really want to be doing right now?
  - Is this who you want to be?
  - If you could do something different, what would it be?
  - What is the likely impact if you carry on?
  - What is the likely impact if you change?

Then decide. The choice is always yours (see the conclusion – **Choices** for more on this)!

The route to WorkJoy – Goals

Using the active WorkJoy formula, let's explore some ideas of how you could use the three Es of Engagement, Energy, and Experimentation within the context of **Goals** to both cultivate WorkJoy and reframe WorkGloom.

Goals	Cultivating WorkJoy	Reframing WorkGloom
Engagement	Consider what type of goal you are trying to set and the approach it might require (**Resolution, Revelation, Revolution, or Evolution?**).	Dig deep to understand what you are holding **limiting beliefs** about and how these are currently limiting your potential.
Energy	Define what you want to achieve using the **PROUD assessment.** Then write it down and invest your energy in the small, manageable steps to get you there.	Decide up front what you're prepared to put in and sacrifice to make it happen, including any **boundaries** you may need to set or adapt.
Experimentation	Try out the different **habit hacks** to work with your brain when you want to build new helpful (and joyful!) habits.	Experiment with working through the five-step **limiting-belief buster** process that will take you from where you are towards integrated helpful habits.

You've now reached the final stages of this toolkit. Let's head into the final chapter and look at how the **Choices** you make will help you to build more joy into your working life.

CHOICES

Introduction

Well done on making it through to the final step! You've now worked through:

- What WorkJoy and WorkGloom are, the **WorkJoy mindset** and the **WorkJoy formulae** (chapter 1)
- The inner WorkJoy factors, including:
  - Your approach to how work fits into your **Life** (chapter 2)
  - The **Values** you hold and how they guide your thinking and behaviours (chapter 3)
  - Your **Boundaries** and how they can enable you to focus your time (chapter 4)
  - The **Stories** you tell yourself and others (chapter 5)
  - Your approach to **Learning** and growth (chapter 6)
- The outer WorkJoy factors, including:
  - The people in your **Squads** who support and challenge you (chapter 7)
  - Your **Career** so far and the shape you might want it to take (chapter 8)
  - The **Organizations** you work with and their influence (chapter 9)
  - Your **Boss** and their impact on you (chapter 10)
- Making it happen, including:
  - The **Goals** you want to work towards (chapter 11)

In this final chapter, you'll look at the choices that you make, perhaps deciding to let some things go. You'll also focus on connecting the dots between what you've learnt on your journey to more WorkJoy. Finally, you'll think about what happens next.

Let's start with this question of choices.

Making choices

Ultimately, creating and cultivating joy in your working life is about making choices. This theme is instilled across all the tools in this kit. Your ability to create and cultivate more joy in your working life will be enhanced if you choose to:

- Notice the good stuff rather than focusing attention on the things that aren't so good
- Reset your expectations into reality rather than the fantasy of perfection
- Direct your energy towards action and experimentation rather than inaction and procrastination
- Create boundaries that allow you to spend time on what's important in your life rather than being pulled in many different directions
- Identify the potential joy in any situation rather than focusing on the gloom
- Re-craft the stories you tell yourself rather than believe them all to be true
- Take personal responsibility for your joy rather than allowing other people to control it for you
- Craft your own career path rather than following the predefined routes
- Evolve your thinking and actions, in small steps over time rather than assuming everything can change overnight
- Let stuff go, creating space for new or different things rather than sticking on the gloomy path

And on that final one, let's explore how you might go about letting some things go.

Letting things go

To create space for joy in your life, you might need to let some things go. The things that no longer serve you, that you've been carrying around, weighing you down. These may be things in your mind, like the stories you've been telling yourself that are now out of date, or your expectations that are set beyond reach, or even your attitude towards how much time you need to build joy. If you're carrying around battered old baggage, you have no room for luxury new luggage, etched with your initials, designed to your own specifications, and created with your personal values in mind. Luggage filled with things you care about, packed with the tools that help you live a more joyful life. The wheels are strong and help you glide over the hurdles in your way. It's light enough to carry round with you and strong enough to withstand life's challenges.

 Reflection questions

- What might you need to let go of?
- How has this helped you up until this point?
- What will be different when you have let this go?

Taking those thoughts, consider using one of these three activities to help you let things go.

Throw it away

This action is for anything that needs to 'be gone' from your thinking/actions:

- Write what you need to let go of on a piece of paper

- Include why you need to let it go (what will be better when it's gone)
- Thank it for how it helped you get to where you are now
- Screw it up, tear it up, shred it, and throw it away
- Tell yourself it is now gone
- Repeat as often as needed (this is not a miracle cure)!

Press pause

For something you might want to come back to but don't want to overthink/worry about/spend time on right now:

- Write what you need to leave for now on a piece of paper
- Include why and when you might want to pick it back up
- Find a box, a file, a place where it can't be easily accessed
- Put the piece of paper in the box, write on the outside a date before which you cannot access it
- Now leave it alone until the set date
- When that date comes, make a choice as to whether to re-open or not

Chat it out

For anything that you need help with:

- Find a trusted colleague, friend, adviser, or a member of your squad
- Talk about what it is you want to let go of
- Ask for help and support
- Take their advice
- Use them as your accountability partner

Connecting the dots

As you enter the final pages of this toolkit, take some time to reflect on the thoughts and activities suggested in this book using the summary of each chapter below. Allow yourself to think them through deeply and get fully immersed. You can choose to:

- Simply reflect on these statements and allow your mind to wonder
- Write down your statements that complete the sentences
- Film yourself answering these questions
- Ask one of your squaddies to chat them through with you
- Use your creativity and draw/paint/sketch (any art form of your choice)

 WorkJoy WorkBook

There's a template for the Connecting the Dots activity in the WorkJoy WorkBook

WorkJoy	Life
• My personal definition of WorkJoy is…	• My important balloons are…
• I have clarity on the things that bring me WorkJoy, and they are…	• I have clarity on what I want the space in-between for and that is…
• I am clear on the things that bring me WorkGloom, and they are…	• I'm working on my wellbeing by…

Values	Boundaries
• My top values are… • I have clarity on what my purpose/s is/are and it is/they are… • I'm working on balancing my values by…	• My non-negotiable, bouncy, and free-flex boundaries are… • I have clarity on what my boundaries will enable me to do and that is… • I'm learning to say no when…
Stories • My core narrative goes a bit like this… • I have clarity on who to share my story with and they are… • I'm working on these bits of my story…	**Learning** • My focus on learning will be in the direction of… • I have clarity on where to invest my development energy and that is… • I'm adding micro-learning into my day by…
Squads • My squad has strength in the following squaddie roles… • I have clarity on where I need to develop my squad and that is… • I'm playing this role in someone else's squad…	**Careers** • My next career move is likely to be shaped like… • I have clarity on whether I stay or go and it's likely I'll… • I'm working on my nextstep readiness by…
Organizations • My organization offers me… • I have clarity on the strengths I bring to the organization, and they are… • I'm currently working through these organizational challenges…	**Bosses** • My boss is great at… • I have clarity on the expectations I have of my boss, and they are… • I'm working through these challenges with my boss…

Goals	Choices
• My goals are focused on achieving… • I have clarity on the hurdles that may thwart my progress and they are… • I'm building helpful habits by…	• I am choosing to cultivate more joy in my life by taking these actions… • I am choosing to manage my WorkGloom by… • I am ready for the next steps because…

Final thoughts – What are you waiting for?

Progress is made in thinking big and acting small. Always remember that you have the choice to create and cultivate more joy in your working life, you don't have to wait for someone else to create it for you. You now have access to tools, activities, and experiments to help you make it happen – start somewhere and see where it leads you. You cannot fail at creating WorkJoy, as you're not aiming for perfection, you're aiming for progress. Every step you take will either move you towards more joy or give you a valuable lesson in what doesn't work for you. You can give yourself permission to embark on this adventure, to invest in it, and to make great things happen for yourself – and by the power of JoyMosis (the unconscious process of sharing joy) you'll bring more joy to the people around you too.

What will you do next?

Now is the time to set yourself an intention to create more joy. Make it small, make it something you can start work on right now. An experiment to try out. An adventure to embark on. A quest to bake more WorkJoy into your life, every single day. Have fun trying things out, the process should feel joyful.

HOW TO STAY CONNECTED

Thank you for working your way through this toolkit. Whether you've taken in every step or pick-and-mixed your way through, I hope it has been useful to you. As I get my WorkJoy kicks from helping you get yours, I'd love to hear about your stories as you engage your thinking, invest your energy, and experiment your way to more WorkJoy.

Email – you can email me on hello@createworkjoy.com or beth@bethstallwood.com

Website – https://createworkjoy.com is where you'll find the latest info, blog, and downloads, including the *free* **WorkJoy WorkBook**. You can find out more about me and my wider work here: https://bethstallwood.com

Podcast – head to your favourite podcast app and search for **the WorkJoy Jam** to hear me interview a diverse range of people about their routes to WorkJoy

Socials – follow and engage with @createworkjoy for thoughts, inspiration, and ideas

I'm excited to hear how you get on!

Beth

WORKING WITH ME

If you're interested in working with me, I offer the following services:

For individuals	For organizations
One-to-one coaching	Keynote talks
Small group coaching	People / HR consulting
Coaching programmes	Facilitation
Self-study programmes	Executive coaching
Head to https://createworkjoy.com to find out more or email me hello@createworkjoy.com	Head to https://bethstallwood.com to find out more or email me beth@bethstallwood.com

ACKNOWLEDGEMENTS

I had been thinking about writing a book for many years and then I was introduced to the wonderful Alison Jones at Practical Inspiration Publishing (thanks to the brilliant Cath Bishop). I signed up to the 10-Day Business Book Challenge to see if the little seed of an idea I was calling WorkJoy had any legs. From creating the WorkJoy Jam podcast (thank you to all my guests who continue to inspire me), to the WorkJoy Way Coaching Programme, Club WorkJoy (a wonderful community) and now this book – it all began in those magical 10 days. Thank you, Alison, for helping me to grow the idea and to all the PIP team for turning it into a real-life book!

A very special thank you goes to Tom Russell at Inky Thinking who provided the illustrations. You turned my dodgy drawings into inspirational images – pieces of art that bring life to the words. They bring me joy every time I look at them. To my amazing story tellers, who dived in and trusted in me to guide them towards more WorkJoy. Abi B, Abi T, Becky, Diane, Helen, Michelle, Stuart, and Tay, I'm honoured that you have chosen to share your personal journeys with the world.

My gratitude goes out to my beta readers, whose input on the draft manuscript breathed life into it when I didn't know what to do next. Thank you, Chris, Janie, Jo, Jordan, Josie, and Kate. I'd also like to give a big verbal hug to Lizzy, who helped me to take it from overly verbose to perhaps just a few too many words? And to Chet, who checked in on my word count progress every Friday for nearly six months – offering a carrot or a baguette (nearest emoji to a stick!) when I needed it.

Big thanks go to my wonderful WorkJoy Team, who make it all possible. Ellie, who enables me to maintain my bouncy boundaries; Becky, who makes me less scared of social media; Dan, for making things look beautiful; Will, for all things webby; Simon – Hey, Mr Podcast Producer; and Kelly, for your creativity in designing the WorkJoy brand. You're all ace and I couldn't do any of it without you.

A note of thanks to the bosses along the way who enabled me to find my WorkJoy and share it with others. Sam, who saw something in a very green 21-year-old, giving me my first experience of learning and development (I was hooked from day one). To Ian, Jenny, and Jon, who cared about work being human (and truly lived the WorkJoy mindset). To Sarah, Karen, and Baljit, who were always up for letting me do things a little differently (and what a collection of powerhouse female leaders!). And a very special shout-out goes to my last boss, Vicky, who gave me incredible challenges to lead and made me brave enough to leave a job I loved to create the business I desired (and has been in my squad ever since).

Big thanks go to Chris, who has been there, quietly, and steadfastly cheering me on in whatever my latest project is, and to my fur-baby Mabel, who brings me more joy than I ever thought possible. Finally, to my wonderful friends who checked in on how it's going and said they were excited to read it, you really kept me going!

INDEX